evaluation basics

evaluation basics

a practitioner's manual

Jacqueline Kosecoff and Arlene Fink

SAGE PUBLICATIONS
Beverly Hills / London / New Delhi

For information address:

SAGE Publications, Inc.
275 South Beverly Drive
Beverly Hills, California 90212

SAGE Publications India Pvt. Ltd.
C-236 Defence Colony
New Delhi 110 024, India

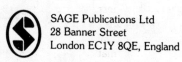

SAGE Publications Ltd
28 Banner Street
London EC1Y 8QE, England

Printed in the United States of America

Library of Congress Cataloging in Publication Data

Kosecoff, Jacqueline B.
   Evaluation basics.

   Bibliography: p.
   1. Evaluation—Handbooks, manuals, etc.   I. Fink,
Arlene.   II. Title
AZ191.K67   1982   001.4   82-16852
ISBN 0-8039-1896-8
ISBN 0-8039-1897-6 (pbk.)

FIRST PRINTING

CONTENTS

LIST OF FIGURES

ACKNOWLEDGMENTS

We would like to thank John D. Wills and Emily Harris of Capitol Publications, Arlington, Virginia, for their generous permission to reprint the monthly newsletters, *How To Evaluate Health Problems*. Many of the ideas, statements, and examples in this book are taken directly from them. It should be emphasized that our clearest thinking reflects Emily Harris's editing and prose. She is truly a gracious employer and a dear friend.

INTRODUCTION

THIS BOOK IS DESIGNED FOR people who conduct program evaluations themselves, work with or for someone else who does, or plan to do so in the future. During the past decade, the technology of evaluation—how it's done—has grown substantially, and the job of evaluator has expanded. Present-day evaluators can no longer be content to be like their predecessors of the 1960s (and even 1970s), relying solely on knowledge of evaluation theory, research design, statistics, and psychometrics. We must negotiate with the scores of people in public and private agencies who finance evaluation studies, put the programs together, and participate in them. We must also organize and administer projects, speak to groups of people, and write proposals, reports and budgets. Finally, evaluators must frequently play the roles of politician and philosopher. By now, we've all accepted the fact that evaluation studies are conducted in a political context, with people within the program competing for power and those outside it competing for money. We also know that we must think as ethicists when we ask personal questions on survey forms (to be sure we don't violate the privacy of the individual) or contemplate random assignment (thereby potentially denying services to some people).

In recognition of the complexity of the evaluator's job and of the possibility that many practitioners might not have yet perfected all the needed skills, we offer some techniques that have proven useful in our work. These techniques are presented in a "how to" format, with step-by-step directions and illustrations.

The approach to evaluation we follow maintains that evaluation is a set of procedures for appraising a program's merit and providing information about its goals, expectations, outcomes (planned for and not anticipated), impact, and costs. With this approach in mind, we have provided techniques for performing various evaluation tasks.

Planning and Management (Chapter II) will tell you how to:

- conduct a needs assessment
- fiscally and administratively manage an evaluation study
- ensure that your evaluation produces scientifically sound and reliable information

Setting Standards (Chapter III) will tell you how to:

- set evaluation standards
- set minimum competency levels of performance

Designing Evaluations and Selecting Samples (Chapter IV) will tell you how to:

- distinguish among three basic designs (case, time series, and comparison group)
- how to sample participants

Collecting Information (Chapter V) will tell you how to:

- select among a range of information collection techniques
- validate data collection strategies
- monitor fieldwork
- construct and use achievement tests, multiple-choice items, questionnaires, interviews, and simulations
- evaluate attitudes

Analyzing Information (Chapter VI) will tell you how to:

- choose and use data analysis techniques
- use ANOVA
- use the Mann-Whitney *U* test
- use chi-square tests
- use pattern analysis

Writing and Reporting (Chapter VII) will tell you how to:

- organize an evaluation report
- write in readable English
- find evaluation references

We hope that in using this book, you will consider the possibility that the unique characteristics of your program might alter some of the applications of our techniques. Consider it as a kind of guidebook that encourages you to make some explorations on your own. We also hope that our omissions are not too disconcerting, and we look forward to a subsequent volume in which we can make up for any shortcomings.

—*Jacqueline Kosecoff*
—*Arlene Fink*

CHAPTER I

An Approach to Program Evaluation

THIS CHAPTER DESCRIBES THE APPROACH to evaluation supported in this book. In subsequent chapters, specific methods for accomplishing various evaluation tasks are given. An understanding of this approach will enable you to use these methods more easily.

The growth of program evaluation as a discipline can be linked to the commitment to use public money to create programs for alleviating social, health, and educational problems. With the proliferation of human services programs from World War II through the 1960s, government and concerned citizens began to request systematic, data-based evaluations of the merits of these programs. Were they truly solving problems? Were they worth the effort? Were all their outcomes beneficial?

To answer these questions, a number of behavioral scientists labored to perfect methods that could be used to provide sound evidence about the worth of social experiments. The 1960s witnessed the publication of many works that enhanced the discipline of evaluation and created a new vocabulary for it. Campbell and Stanley's (1963) monograph on experimental and quasi-experimental research designs, for example, has become a cornerstone of evaluation practice. In 1967, Scriven introduced the concepts of "formative" and "summative" evaluation and produced a new perspective on the purposes of evaluation research. Donabedian (1969), concerned with assessing the quality of medical care, added the ideas of structure, process, and outcome to the evaluator's conceptual arsenal.

In the 1970s and 1980s new theoretical and practical understanding furthered the growth and development of social program evaluation (Caro, 1970; Weiss, 1972; Gutentag and Struening, 1975; Fink and Kosecoff, 1978; Cronbach et al., 1980; Rossi and Freeman, 1982).

In recognizing the importance of evaluation, most federal government agencies require that an evaluation component be included in the plan of a human services program. The Office of Education, the National Institute of Education, the General Accounting Office, the National Institute of Mental Health, the National Cancer Institute, and various professional organizations have also sponsored the preparation of evaluation standards and guidelines. Nevertheless, the debate over the significance of evaluation and evaluation research is by no means resolved and continues to be lively. Should qualitative or quantitative methods and data be used (Patton, 1980)? Is evaluation research obsolete (Dunn et al., 1981)?

The debate and the questions tend to get published more often than the hundreds of evaluation studies that have been conducted with useful results. But we believe that the answers to the questions are probably also dependent on one's beliefs about the extent to which society is willing to make decisions about its problems by relying on systematically obtained data (rather than on pure intuition or past practices) and the ability of evaluation to provide society with the needed information. Our position is that evaluations are more than capable of producing valid information, and that untold numbers of programs and policies in health, education, law, and other social services have been changed because of them.

WHO CONDUCTS EVALUATIONS?

Evaluation is a set of procedures to appraise a program's merit and to provide information about its goals, expectations, activities, outcomes, impact, and costs. Evaluations are conducted because groups or individuals want to know about a program's progress and/or effectiveness. The board of directors of a philanthropic foundation, for example, might ask as a condition for its support that evidence be provided that a health education program is actually changing children's knowledge and behavior in a beneficial way, although the teachers in the program might only want data on how well their own students are performing with respect to specific lessons. Evaluations are thus considered to have significance in that they produce useful information, although other considerations, such as social need and the availability of money and skilled staff, may also be influential in helping to decide the fate of a program.

Because evaluation data are thought to derive their value from their usefulness to program developers, sponsors, and future consumers, only rarely are evaluation studies conducted for the primary purpose of contributing new knowledge to a field (the major aim of other kinds of social research). It would be very unusual for the sponsors of an evaluation of a health education program, for example, to support a study whose basic purpose was to test hypotheses about learning and teaching instead of to describe and assess the effects of program participation.

Evaluations can make certain scholarly contributions in that they can add to the store of knowledge about innovative programs. In fact, the main concern of evaluation research is a program or a systematic effort to achieve certain expectations and change behavior, attitudes, and thought. Other kinds of research usually do not consider programs, but concentrate instead on problems, issues, or theories. Although the lines between evaluations and other kinds of research sometimes become blurred, a study that focuses on providing data about a program's merit or worth to prespecified individuals or agencies is likely to be evaluation research.

The audiences for evaluation and other kinds of applied social research also differ. Since evaluations focus on the provision of data about programs, the consumers of evaluation information tend to be involved directly with the program itself or with other, somewhat similar, interventions, or they are concerned with the social welfare the program is supposed to promote. The users of research findings, however, tend to have much broader backgrounds and interests and are drawn from the entire scholarly and lay communities. Because of their limited audience, evaluations rarely get published; hence, the audience remains limited.

Scientifically rigorous evaluations use the same standards to select their methods as do other applied research studies. Unfortunately, evaluations do not always achieve the high levels of technical soundness many advocate for them, a condition evaluators often and publicly lament. This is especially true of relatively small programs whose financial resources are severely restricted, or when the need for information is immediate, leaving no real time for extensive investigations.

Take the issue of research design, for example. Although it is generally asserted that the strongest evaluation studies make comparisons between at least two groups (one of which has received the innovative program or services while the other has not), one of the perennial problems faced by evaluators is the inaccessibility of control groups. Experience has shown that finding a control group (say, a second health education program with aims that are similar to the one being evaluated) is extremely difficult. Also, the best comparison groups for evaluation studies are those that are constituted randomly. But the problems of randomization (e.g., how to keep the students in education program A at school X from talking to students in education program B in the same school, thereby confounding the effects of each) are sometimes nearly impossible to overcome.

Another problem that can work against thoroughly rigorous evaluation studies is the relative unavailability of reliable and valid instruments to measure changes in behavior, attitudes, and knowledge. Good measures of perception, attitude, and values, for example, are extremely difficult to find, and although it is possible to develop them, the process by which a valid measure is produced requires considerable psychometric expertise, time, and money, all of which are often in short supply.

AN APPROACH TO EVALUATION

Despite these difficulties, credible evaluations are more than possible. The technology for conducting them has become reasonably sophisticated in the past decade and is relatively accessible. Evaluations usually include five major activities: formulating questions and standards, selecting designs and sampling procedures, collecting information, analyzing information, and reporting information.

Formulating Questions and Standards

Evaluation questions are the focus of any rigorous evaluation. They define the evaluation consumer's need and set the study's boundaries. Some typical evaluation questions include:

- How well did the program achieve its goals, hopes, or expectations?
- Were the program's activities implemented as planned?
- For which groups was the program most/least successful?
- What social and political effects did the program have?
- What did the program cost?

The evaluation questions should not be the evaluator's questions. They should come instead from those who commission the evaluation or who must use the evaluation information. In some cases, getting agreement on which questions to ask is relatively simple; in others, it is more difficult. In a few instances, the questions may be chosen long before the evaluation, say, at the time of program planning. When this happens, the evaluator should check to be sure that the questions are still important and that no new ones need to be added. Occasionally, the evaluation questions are mandated by law. To ensure valid evaluation questions, the evaluator should become familiar with the program, its sponsors, and its participants, and include them in the question-formulating process whenever possible.

Setting evaluation standards means deciding what kind of information will provide convincing evidence of a program's success. A program is usually considered successful if the answers to the evaluation questions are positive in that goals, hopes, or expectations are achieved, and activities are implemented as planned with beneficial, economical results.

Evaluation standards can also be set by measuring improvement. Standards based on improvement are relatively easy to understand and quantify, but it is sometimes difficult to decide just how much improvement is truly meaningful.

Finally, the evaluator may be able to employ established practice or norms. Established practice provides easily understood evidence of program merit, but relying on it sometimes means overlooking regional variations in needs, costs, and resources. There is also the possibility that standards may not be meaningful for a particular program and sometimes, normative data are simply not available.

Selecting Designs and Sampling Procedures

A design describes how to group people to answer evaluation questions. Sometimes a single design can be used to answer all the questions in an evaluation; sometimes, several designs are needed. A classic example of a design strategy is one in which the participants are separated into two groups; one group is given an experimental program, and the other group, a placebo program.

Evaluators use internal and external validity as the criteria for deciding how accurately a design strategy will answer the evaluation questions. When a design has internal validity, it is possible to distinguish between changes caused by the program being evaluated and changes resulting from other causes. If an evaluation were comparing two programs for the elderly, the example, it would be difficult to tell whether variations in levels of compliance with a drug regimen each year were due to the programs or to preexisting differences among people, with some being generally more cooperative than others. Such a design may lack internal validity.

External validity measures whether an evaluation's findings will hold true for other people in other places. If participants perform better simply because they are excited about taking part in an innovative program (the Hawthorne Effect), the evaluation may lack external validity.

All designs must be internally valid. External validity is important whenever an evaluation's findings are going to be applied to people or settings that were not included in the evaluation, or when findings based on current participants will be used to make decisions affecting future participants.

Collecting Information

The collection of evaluation information is really a set of tasks that includes identifying what is to be measured (the dependent variable); selecting, adapting, or developing a strategy or instruments for measurement; administering those measurements; and scoring and interpreting the results. The crux of the data collection effort is to obtain reliable and valid information. Reliable data are consistent over time, while valid data are also accurate and truly reflect the concepts, ideas, or purposes being evaluated. Many of of the hoped-for outcomes of social programs have proven difficult to define or measure. For example, how is one to capture a group's or an individual's attitudes, values, feelings, or hopes? Also, what constitutes valid evidence that a program produced good doctors, teachers, lawyers, or citizens? Information collection also raises ethical concerns. For instance, when does measurement become simple prying?

Despite the problems, evaluators do have a battery of instruments and strategies for collecting data. These include questionnaires, observations, interviews, written achievement or competency tests, performance tests, record reviews, and diaries.

Analyzing Information

Data analysis is the evaluator's way of describing and explaining information. Analytic techniques for evaluation range from the statistical methods of experimental psychologists and epidemiologists to the scholarship methods of historians and anthropologists. All attempt to describe evaluation information by tallies or frequency counts, summaries, averages, and measures of variation and range. They also explain information by comparing groups, identifying patterns and trends, and establishing relationships among variables.

The evaluation questions are the evaluator's guide for selecting an analytic technique suited to a particular study. For example, consider the following examples:

- How does the XYZ program differ from the ABC program in promoting good health habits in young children?

- How does the XYZ program differ from the RST program in promoting good health habits in young children, encouraging parent involvement, and gaining teacher acceptance?

- Is there a relationship between birth order and success in the XYZ program?

The first two questions ask the evaluator to describe differences between programs. The first question asks only about health habits, while the second question includes other variables as well. Different analytic techniques may be needed to answer these two questions (perhaps a t test for the first and a multivariate analysis of variance for the second). The third evaluation question asks about a relationship, which requires an analytic technique, such as correlation, that focuses on the association between variables.

Reporting Information

Evaluation reports may be highly informal (a 15-minute talk to the PTA) or formal (a written report of the evaluation's findings and methods). Among the most difficult tasks most evaluators face is describing what they do to someone who still equates evaluation with arbitrary judgment or social science hocus-pocus while, at the same time, demonstrating to others the technical soundness of their methods and the objectivity of their observations.

An additional problem is the variation in types of reports required of evaluators. It is not uncommon for evaluators to produce both written final and program reports for the study's sponsor and simple tables, charts, and summaries for people with different hopes for and interests in the program, all within a short period of time.

It is probably wise for the evaluator to be prepared at almost any time to describe and justify:

- the evaluation questions and limitations on the scope of the evaluation;
- the design strategy, the sampling procedures, and their limitations for each evaluation question;
- the information collection techniques and instruments and their limitations;
- how data were collected and how confidentiality was observed;
- the methods used to analyze the evaluation information, their limitations, and the results for each analysis;
- the answers to each evaluation question, including an interpretation of the findings and a list of recommendations; and
- administrative details such as schedules, staff assignments, and costs.

CHAPTER II

Planning and Management

THIS CHAPTER IS ABOUT ACTIVITIES that an evaluator ought to consider before beginning the evaluation study itself. The first activity is called *needs assessment*, and it should actually be conducted before the program is organized. The purpose of a needs assessment is to identify the goals for which a program should strive, goals that are important to society, not currently being achieved, and potentially feasible. Needs assessment studies have traditionally been performed by evaluators even though such studies are technically part of program planning rather than program appraisal.

The second activity described in this chapter is the *management of evaluation studies*. This activity should begin before the evaluation is implemented, and it continues until the evaluation is completed. Evaluators are typically behavioral or social scientists whose primary responsibility is to produce sound appraisals of program merit. Their work, however, must be accomplished within strict budgetary, time, and personnel restraints. Evaluators must therefore learn how to manage an evaluation, and that includes hiring and monitoring personnel, deciding how to spend staff time, and writing realistic budgets.

The last two sections of this chapter offer sets of guidelines for conducting evaluations that should yield credible and scientifically rigorous results. These guidelines are intended to help you plan your evaluation studies. The first set of guidelines was developed by the Joint Dissemination Review Panel for education programs. The second was prepared for evaluations of health and other social action programs.

HOW TO CONDUCT A NEEDS ASSESSMENT

What is needs assessment? It is the process by which you identify needs and decide on priorities among them. So what is a need? Sometimes it is defined as a condition in which there is a discrepancy between an acceptable state of affairs and an observed state of affairs.

Needs assessment can be done for individuals, groups, or institutions. Here, we will show you a needs assessment method developed by Dr. David Satcher, former acting dean of the King-Drew Medical Center in Los Angeles, as part of the process of setting up a family practice program.

King-Drew is located in the inner-city community of Watts, an area that is well known for being medically underserved. Watts has a lower-than-average income, younger population, higher unemployment rate, and higher death rate than Los Angeles County as a whole. Few primary care services are available to the Watts population. Given the comprehensive nature of family practice services, it seemed that such a program at King-Drew could help the community in many ways.

To find out which of the many potential family practice services the community wanted and needed, and to make efficient use of available resources, the staff of the King-Drew family practice program (chaired by Dr. Satcher) decided to conduct an assessment of the needs of the consumers and the providers in the community. Dr. Satcher's strategy has five steps: identify potential objectives, decide which objectives are most important, assess currently available services, collect information, and select final objectives.

Identify Potential Objectives

Your first step is to compile a comprehensive list of objectives for the program. Go to the experts, the literature, or the community, for examples and suggestions.

In the King-Drew needs assessment, statements of family practice objectives were obtained principally from a literature review. These were mostly primary care objectives for individuals and for families. In addition, the staff obtained objectives from a review of twenty family practice programs located throughout the country.

After the list was compiled, a group composed of two board-certified family physicians, one internist, one epidemiologist, two education specialists, and two consumer advocates met to discuss and refine the findings. They came up with fifty statements of objectives such as the following:

- To teach individuals and families to identify the dangers of common health problems (e.g., lead poisoning, high blood pressure, obesity)
- To reduce the time a patient has to wait to see a doctor
- To identify and assist with family problems that can threaten health, such as child abuse and alcoholism
- To care for normal pregnancies and deliveries

Decide Which Objectives Are Most Important

Next, you should select individuals and groups whose interests and views on health services you consider important. Have them rate the objectives and then combine the results.

In the King-Drew needs assessment, three community groups were identified for participation: consumers (actual or potential users of services), providers, and health care administrators. (The overall sample size for all three groups was 1022.)

- *Consumers:* A sample of 350 households was systematically drawn from a probability sample of 1000 households in the King-Drew service area. The 1000-household sample was representative of the racial, income, educational, housing, and employment characteristics of the service area. To ensure that former or current users of services were included in the consumer sample, three additional subsets were added: (1) a sample of 100 names was systematically selected from a list of participants at monthly Community Medical Forums held at King-Drew; (2) another 100 names were systematically selected from participants in outreach screening programs conducted by King-Drew; (3) a random sample of 150 patients at the Walk-In Clinic was selected and 24 patients were chosen from those attending the Free Clinic. The total sample size for the consumer subsample was 724.

- *Providers:* Providers included in the sample were physicians (staff members at King-Drew and community physicians), nurses, social workers, and MEDEX students. Every third physician (n = 641) on the roster of the center was systematically selected; physicians from all departments and professional ranks were included. Every fifth (n = 100) physician was systematically selected from a list of 500 community practitioners. In addition, 20 social workers, 20 nurses, and 20 MEDEX students were systematically selected from King-Drew. Total sample size for the provider group was 224.

- *Administrators:* Administrators (n = 74) were systematically drawn from top- and middle-level positions at King-Drew.

To decide which objectives were most important, Dr. Satcher's staff asked each individual to complete a questionnaire. It contained statements of objectives with 5-point rating scales, from 1 = least important to 5 = most important. When rating the importance of each objective, the staff asked people to assign at least two objectives to each of the five response categories. This is called a *Q-sort technique.* It is used because people have a tendency to rate all objectives either very high or very low, and this is one way to break that pattern. It helps to ensure that ratings accurately reflect the relative importance of each objective to the respondent.

The directions for rating each objective were:

Rating of importance of services: You will see five possible responses, ranging from "most important" to "least important." For objectives or services you value the highest, please check "most important." For the ones you value least, check "least important." For those in between, check "below average," "average," or "above average." We ask that you follow one rule: You must place at least two of the objectives or services listed in each response category, so that you have at least two rated "most important," two rated "above average importance," and so on. Remember, to rate an objective or service as "least important" does not necessarily mean that you think it isn't important, only that you think it's least important compared to others.

Assess the Nature and Type of Currently Available Services

The third step is to get information about how well your programs are currently meeting their objectives. You might find this information in records or in experimental and evaluation data, or you might try a survey of community experts or citizens.

King-Drew's questionnaire, which asked consumers, providers, and administrators about the importance of family practice objectives, included two additional 3-point rating scales. One was for judging feasibility (Can we do it?); the other was for assessing availability (Are we already doing it?). The purpose of these additional questions was to get an overall picture of the current situation in health services. The King-Drew staff wanted to know whether services rated as important were already available, and if not, whether this was because it was impractical to provide them.

The directions for rating feasibility and availability were:

> *Rating feasibility of services:* Please rate the feasibility of providing this service in the community on a scale that goes from "easy to provide" to "possible to provide, but difficult," to "cannot be provided at this time." Please rate the feasibility of providing these services with the present resources available to this community.

> *Rating availability of services:* Please rate the availability of each objective or service. How easy is it for the community to get the service at this time? The 3-part scale goes from "easily available" to "available, but difficult to get" to "not available as far as I know."

Before coming up with the final version, the King-Drew staff pretested a 50-statement questionnaire (using the preliminary objectives) on a small sample (50) of consumers, providers, and administrators. In addition to the other response choices, the staff added "Do not understand" as a possible choice for each rating scale on the pretest questionnaire.

After looking at the results of the pretest, the staff revised several objectives to make them clearer and less confusing and dropped the ones that appeared difficult to understand. (Note: Consumers in the pretest sample had trouble rating feasibility, so the final questionnaire for consumers used only the importance and availability ratings.) The final questionnaire contained 38 statements of objectives that were representative of the statements on the original list of 50. A Spanish-language translation was prepared for respondents who were more comfortable with that language.

Collect Information

Like the staff at King-Drew, you should consider using questionnaires (or interviews for smaller samples) to collect the needs assessment information. Don't forget to check the accuracy and completeness of the responses. King-Drew used mail questionnaires and supplemented these with questionnaires that people completed with the help of the staff.

Before you use a mail survey, you ought to know what you're getting into. Some people find them an invasion of privacy; others merely find them boring. At King-Drew, there were other problems as well. Although the staff had hoped for a 50% response rate, the actual rate was only 40.77%. They attributed this to the poor response rates of several groups of people.

- Of the 300 questionnaires mailed to consumers, 90 were returned with incorrect addresses. Of the 210 actually delivered, 54 were completed and returned.

- Of the 598 questionnaires mailed all together, 113 were returned with incorrect addresses—90 in the consumer subsample and 23 in the community provider subsample. Recalculating the return rate using the number of questionnaires delivered as the denominator (rather than the number of questionnaires mailed) increased the response rate to 26% for consumers and 41.8% for providers.

- A total of 424 supervised questionnaires were attempted. Of this total, 20 had incorrect addresses, 80 were not at home, and 94 refused to participate.

- Fully 80% of the consumers who responded followed the Q-sort directions to place at least two objectives in each rating category. Among providers and administrators, 90% followed the Q-sort directions.

Select Final Objectives

In the last needs assessment step, you must synthesize information in order to set priorities among objectives. Although complex mathematical models are sometimes used, you will find that relatively simple schemes can produce excellent results. At King-Drew, the staff used a table similar to the one presented in Example 1 to analyze the results.

After studying the table, the King-Drew staff gave top priority to providing services that were rated high in importance, low in availability, and high in feasibility. They decided to conduct further research on other objectives, with priority on services rated low in feasibility, high in importance, and low in availability.

Example 1 Synthesis of Needs Assessment Results

Availability	Feasibility	2.5*-3.5	3.5-4.0	4.0-4.5	4.5-5.0
				Importance	
0.0-2.0	1.0-2.0		Objective No. 20	Objectives No. 4, 6, 38	
	2.0-3.0		Objectives No. 7, 17, 23, 29, 19, 33 36	Objectives No. 5, 31, 22, 25	
2.0-3.0	1.0-2.0	Objectives No. 11, 37			
	2.0	Objective No. 24	Objectives No. 8, 12, 14, 21, 26, 32	Objectives No. 2, 3, 10, 15, 16, 18, 27, 28, 30, 34, 35	Objective No. 1

*No objective's overall importance fell below a mean rating of 2.5.

With this priority system, four objectives were chosen for implementation. Each was rated greater than 4.0 in importance, less than 2.0 in availability, and greater than 2.0 in feasibility. They were:

(No. 5) To set up health services that are close to the people in the community

(No. 22) To identify and assist with family problems that are threats to health

(No. 25) To adequately treat common or frequent health problems in the same clinic

(No. 31) To make better use of community resources

In addition, three objectives received top priority for family practice research. Each was rated less than 2.0 for feasibility, but greater than 4.0 in importance and less than 2.0 for availability. They were:

(No. 4) To reduce the cost of health care

(No. 6) To reduce the time a patient has to wait for health services

(No. 38) To make home visits when indicated

HOW TO MANAGE AN EVALUATION

Evaluation information is perishable. It is essential to coordinate activities so that the right information is ready when needed. If clients don't get answers to their questions in time to make decisions, the evaluation isn't worth much. No matter how large or small an evaluation is, some of your time must be allocated to management. The three most important management functions you will have to perform are establishing schedules, assigning staff and monitoring their activities, and budgeting.

How to Establish Schedules

Evaluations are supposed to be completed within a given amount of time. If you don't finish on time, funds probably won't be available unless you make special arrangements or the evaluation information may be too late to be useful.

It's important to know just when each evaluation activity will take place, the sequence of activities, and how long each activity will last. To do this, you must pay attention to:

- the evaluation activities themselves;
- the deadline for completing each activity; and
- the amount of time to be given to each activity (i.e., the actual number of professional hours, days, or weeks needed, even if they are spread over a longer period of time).

You can combine evaluation activities, deadlines, and time allocations in several ways to create schedules. Examples 2 and 3 illustrate time schedules for managing evaluations. Example 2 lists a beginning and ending date (or deadline) for each activity and specifies the time allocated to it. Example 3 represents a time schedule organized by months. Beginning and ending dates for each activity are joined by a double-arrowheaded line, and the number of days allocated to each activity is shown in parentheses directly under the line.

How to Assign Staff and Monitor Activities

Before you assign staff to specific evaluation activities you should know what skills it takes to perform each activity. Example 4 shows a

Example 2   Excerpt from an Overview of Activities, Staff, and Time Schedules

Activities	Dates	Time Allocation (total days)
(1) Becoming familiar with the program goals, activities, and evidence of program merit, including: • reading all program-related documents and reports; • meeting with program director and staff; • observing program in operation.	3/1/82 to 4/15/82	15
(2) Formulating evaluation questions, including a review by program staff and Advisory Committee.	4/16/82 to 5/31/82	10
(3) Preparing evaluation design strategies and sampling plan.	6/1/82 to 6/30/82	10
(4) Preparing information collection to include field testing.	6/15/82 to 9/30/82	12
(5) Collecting evaluation information.	10/1/82 to 5/30/83	35
(6) Preparing information for analysis.	11/1/82 to 6/15/83	7
(7) Analyzing evaluation information and interpreting the results.	2/1/83 to 7/31/83	14
(8) Preparing preliminary evaluation reports.	8/31/82 to 2/28/83	4
(9) Preparing final evaluation report.	6/1/83 to 8/31/83	22

(continued)

Example 3 Sample Evaluation Schedule

School		Principal Interview Items										Per pupil cost				Text-book cost		
		1	2	3	4	5	6	7	8	9	10							
0	1	1	1	2	2	3	3	1	1	2	1	0	8	8	7	0	5	2
0	2	2	6	5	3	3	4	2	4	2	1	0	9	2	8	0	5	5
0	3	3	2	3	4	3	5	2	3	3	2	1	8	1	8	0	4	2
0	4	4	5	4	4	3	5	1	5	1	3	1	7	6	9	1	9	1
0	5	1	3	4	3	3	7	1	5	1	3	1	5	3	6	5	4	6
0	6	2	4	5	1	3	2	2	5	2	1	0	8	8	6	9	4	9
0	7	3	1	2	2	3	1	1	5	3	2	0	9	9	7	3	1	2
0	8	4	6	5	3	3	3	2	4	1	3	1	4	2	8	3	4	8
0	9	1	2	3	4	3	9	1	3	1	3	1	4	4	9	0	0	6
1	0	2	5	4	3	3	4	9	2	3	2	1	7	6	7	4	2	8
1	1	3	3	4	2	3	3	2	1	2	1	1	7	2	7	5	5	6
1	2	4	4	3	2	3	3	1	3	2	1	1	6	5	7	2	2	3
1	3	1	9	1	9	3	1	9	5	3	9	1	4	3	6	3	1	9
1	4	2	1	2	1	3	5	1	5	9	3	0	9	9	9	3	0	2
1	5	3	6	5	2	3	9	2	9	3	2	0	8	7	9	4	1	6
1	6	4	2	1	1	3	9	1	1	2	1	1	4	4	7	5	3	8

convenient way to summarize staff assignments. This example is organized to show the role each person will play in evaluation and the total amount of time each person will devote to it. Example 5 is arranged

Example 4 Sample Staff Allocation Chart

Staff Assignment	Title/Role	Percentage Time
Dr. Leroy Samuels	Evaluation Director	50 ✓
Dr. Susan Baker	Instrument Development	15
Dr. Sharon Hathway	Information Collection	50
Ms. Gretel Burry	Information Analysis	20
Mr. James Wardling	Research Associate	100
Mr. Harry Vivell	Secretary	25

according to activity. It is the same as Example 2 except that it has been enlarged to show the specific amount of time to be spent on each activity by each staff member.

Managing an evaluation of a health or social action program also means you will have to keep an eye on how efficiently your staff performs the evaluation activities. You should collect information about the amount of time spent on each activity, how thoroughly it has been accomplished, and any problems encountered. This information can be collected in several ways, ranging from highly structured reporting systems to informal meetings with staff members.

How to Budget

An evaluation is usually allotted a given amount of money with which to work, and must be completed without exceeding that amount. To prepare the budget, you must weigh what needs to be done against what you have to do, juggling activities, time allocations, and staff assignments according to the amount of money and time available. For some evaluations you will find the budget already laid out for you in detail; for others you will be allowed to design your own.

The sample budget in Example 6 includes items required by most state and federal agencies and foundations that support health, education, and welfare programs. Note the distinction between direct and indirect costs. *Direct costs* are staff and nonstaff costs related to a particular evaluation. For example, the salaries and expenses of secretaries or clerks who work for the evaluation are charged as direct costs according to the amount of time they actually spend on the evaluation. *Indirect costs* are expenses that are not directly related to

(text continues on p. 42)

Example 5   Sample Overview of Activities, Dates, Staff, and Time Allocations

Activities	Dates	Staff Assignments	Time Allocated By Staff	Total Days
(1) Becoming familiar with the program's goals, activities, and evidence of program merit including: ● reading all program-related documents and reports; ● meeting with program director and staff; ● observing program in operation.	3/1/82 to 4/15/82	Smith Ramirez Goldberg	10 2 3	15
(2) Formulating evaluation questions, including a review by program staff and Advisory Committee.	4/16/82 to 5/31/82	Smith Ramirez Goldberg	7 2 1	10
(3) Preparing evaluation design strategies and sampling plan.	6/1/82 to 6/30/82	Smith Ramirez Goldberg	2 7 1	10

Activity	Dates	Staff		Total
(4) Preparing information collection, including field testing.	6/15/82 to 6/30/82	Cheung Smith Ramirez Goldberg	3 2 7 1	12
(5) Collecting evaluation information.	10/1/82 to 5/30/83	Smith Goldberg Cheung	3 12 20	35
(6) Preparing information for analysis.	11/1/82 to 6/15/83	Smith Ramirez	1 6	7
(7) Analyzing evaluation information and interpreting the results.	2/1/83 to 7/31/83	Smith Ramirez	3 11	14
(8) Preparing preliminary evaluation reports.	8/31/82 to 2/28/83	Smith	4	4
(9) Preparing final evaluation reports.	6/1/83 to 8/31/83	Smith Ramirez Goldberg Cheung	7 6 6 3	22

Example 6   Sample Budget

Direct Costs

Divide your costs into staff and nonstaff sections.

I. Staff

    A. Salaries and Wages

List here the salaries and wages of full-time and part-time persons employed for the evaluation at a rate proportionate to their efforts on the evaluation. For each staff position, provide the following information: number of persons at that position, their title, daily, monthly or annual salary, percentage of time on the evaluation, number of months employed, and the total dollar figure.

Example A–Salaries and Wages

(1) Dr. Peter Korn, Evaluation Director (20% time at $24,000 per year; 2/1/82-1/31/83)	$ 4,800
(2) Ms. Maureen Malarophy, Information Analysis (35% time at $24,000 per year; 3/1/82-5/31/82; 9/15/82-12/14/82)	4,200
(3) Dr. Ralph Heffer, Instrumentation (25% time at $24,000 per year; 2/1/82-7/31/82)	4,200
(4) Dr. Susan Schrager, Field Research (25% time at $15,000 per year; 2/1/82-1/31/83)	5,250
(5) Secretary/Clerical Assistant (50% time at $8,400 per year; 2/1/82-1/31/83)	4,200
Subtotal	$22,650

    B. Employee Benefits

Show the costs of all employee benefits related to the salaries and wages of full-time and part-time staff. Benefits are usually computed as a percentage of salaries and wages and include funds set aside by the employer for social security, retirement, medical care, and so on. Sometimes each type of benefit is listed separately.

Example B–Employee Benefits

(1) 16% of salaries and wages ($22,650)	$ 3,624

    C. Consultants

Consultants are persons who are hired on an as-needed basis such as reviewers, members of an advisory panel, subject matter experts, or fieldworkers.

Example C–Consultants

(1) Members of Advisory Panel (9 persons @ $125 per day for 2 days each)	$ 2,250

Example 6 (Continued)

II. Nonstaff

A. Rent

Show here the cost of using facilities for the evaluation, including utilities and maintenance services.

Example A—Office Space

(1) Office space (250 sq. ft. @ 40¢ per sq. ft., $100 per $ 1,200
month for 12 months)

B. Office Supplies

List consumable supplies used exclusively for the project, like paper, typewriter ribbons, and so on.

Example B—Office Supplies

(1) Office supplies (paper, etc.) at $50 per month $ 600
for 12 months

C. Equipment

Specify the cost of equipment acquired or rented for specific use on the project, like typewriters, photocopy machines, and so on.

Example C—Equipment

(1) Rental of typewriters and photocopy machines $ 1,000
for 12 months

D. Computer Use

List computer time and necessary supporting services.

Example D—Computer Use

(1) Computer time $ 3,000

(2) Data processing supplies (tape, cards, keypunching) $ 500

E. Telephone and Mail

Show costs of telephone services, phone calls, postage.

Example E—Telephone and Mail

(1) Telephone and mail @ $50 per month for 12 months $ 600

F. Printing and Reproduction

List costs of photocopying, typesetting, duplicating reports, and so on.

Example F—Printing and Reproduction

(1) Printing (questionnaires, observation schedules, $ 1,200
reports)

(2) Reproduction @ $15 per month for 12 months $ 180

(continued)

Example 6 (Continued)

II. Nonstaff (Cont.)

G. Travel

   Show all travel charges incurred for the project, including the per-day expenses, gas mileage, airfare.

   Example G – Travel

   (1) Travel to sites (9 trips @ $300 per trip) $ 2,700

Indirect Costs

You may compute indirect costs as a percentage of the total direct costs or as a percentage of salaries and wages. Usually, indirect costs include expenses for general administrative services (bookkeeping, personnel, payroll, and so on).

Example – Indirect Costs

Indirect Costs = 22% of Direct Costs ($39,504) $ 8,690.88

---

the particular evaluation but that contribute to the evaluation agency's continued existence. Expenses for secretaries or clerks who keep your office running would probably be incorporated into the indirect costs.

Once you have completed your sample budget, you can transform it into a conventional budget format as illustrated in Example 7.

HOW TO PROVE A PROGRAM WORKS

The Joint Dissemination Review Panel was created by the Department of Health, Education and Welfare to review education programs developed with federal funds. The rigorous standards that the panel (which is now part of the national Diffusion Network) set for evaluation practices are, in our view, valid for most programs, and if adhered to, likely to produce excellent studies.

Try the following steps to see whether your program and its evaluation measure up to the rigorous standards of the Joint Dissemination Review Panel (Tallmadge, 1977).

Did a Change Occur?

Your first effort should be to identify and describe important results that are directly and logically related to the purposes of the program.

Example 7   Detailed Budget for a 12-Month (260-day) Evaluation from 2/1/82 to 1/31/83

DIRECT COSTS

I. Staff

A. Salaries and Wages and Benefits

Name	Title	Time (Days)	Salary	Benefits	Total
1. Dr. Peter Korn	Director	52	4,800	768	5,568
2. Ms. Maureen Malarophy	Information Analyst	45-1/2	4,200	672	4,872
3. Dr. Ralph Heffer	Instrumentation	45-1/2	4,200	672	4,872
4. Dr. Susan Schrager	Field Research	91	5,250	840	6,090
5. To Be Named	Secretary/Clark	130	4,200	672	4,872
		Subtotal	$22,650	$3,624	$26,274

B. Consultants

    1. Members of Advisory Panel (9 persons @ $125 per day for 2 days each)   2,250

II. Nonstaff

A. Rent
    1. Office Space (250 square feet at 40¢ per sq. ft. = $100 per month)   1,200

B. Office Supplies
    1. Office Supplies (paper, etc.) at 50¢ per month for 12 months   600

C. Equipment
    1. Rental of Typewriters and Photocopy Machine at $88.33 per month for 12 months   1,000

D. Computer Use
    1. Computer Time   3,000
    2. Data Processing Supplies (tapes, cards, keypunching, etc.)   500

E. Telephone and Mail
    1. Telephone and Mail at $50 per month for 12 months   600

F. Printing and Reproduction
    1. Printing (questionnaires, observation schedules, reports)   1,200
    2. Reproduction at $15 per month for 12 months   180

G. Travel
    1. Travel to Sites (9 trips at $300 per trip)   2,700

        Subtotal Nonstaff Costs $10,980

INDIRECT COSTS

22% of Direct Costs ($39,504)   8,691

        Grand Total $48,195

Which outcomes are central to the program's success? Which ones may be important but not crucial? Which ones are interesting but not particularly important? Look for evidence of changes that match the central objectives of the program. Here's an example:

Example 8   Polio Inoculation

A large prepaid health system with many hospitals discovered that children of migrant workers were not being inoculated against polio. Health system officials thought one reason might be that the children didn't live in one place long enough to benefit from a total pediatric care program. They decided to try a special program to provide copies of each patient's chart simultaneously in every hospital. They also began giving special attention to migrant families.

The central evidence of change would probably be a better rate of inoculation (based on a chart review) and a lower incidence of polio. Evidence of better overall health care would be considered an important supporting element, but not central to the program's purpose. Evidence of satisfaction with the program among migrant families might not be considered important enough to include in an evaluation report.

Once you have identified the central evidence you need, the next step is to find it. In other words, you have to prove that something changed as a result of the program.

To prove that a change occurred, you must have *valid and reliable measures* of conditions after the intervention has had time to take effect. You must also have estimates of what would have happened (at that same point in time) if there had been no intervention at all. Valid and reliable measures are instruments that assess with consistency and accuracy exactly what the program is trying to achieve. The surest way to demonstrate the effects of the intervention is to use true experimental designs; sometimes, quasi-experimental designs with comparison groups are also used.

The following is an example of unconvincing evidence of change, one that might leave the Joint Dissemination Review Panel skeptical:

Example 9   The Marina City Veterans Administration's Drug Abuse Program

The Marina City Veterans Administration has a new drug abuse prevention program. Evaluators formed a control group by identifying one group of veterans and matching them to another in terms of sex, age, and past history of drug use. To measure anxiety, a central program variable, they developed a 10-item questionnaire, which they administered monthly to veterans in both groups.

Why is the evidence obtained in this way unconvincing?

(1) Anxiety is a psychological trait that can only be measured with an instrument that has demonstrated construct validity.

(2) Getting a control group by matching people with those in an experimental program is not a preferred strategy.

To obtain more convincing evidence, try this:

Example 10   Drug Abuse Continued

One-half of all eligible veterans are randomly selected to participate in the program while the other half are assigned to a program control group. The XYZ Anxiety Inventory is administered to all veterans in both groups once a month. This instrument has been field tested extensively and found to have high construct validity and test/retest reliability. In addition, a psychiatrist interviews a random sample of 20% of the program and control veterans to assess their psychological states.

What makes the evidence here so persuasive? You obtained it from more than one source and you used rigorous methods to get it.

Was the Effect Statistically Significant?

To be convincing, the program must include large numbers of people or be tried out often enough with small samples to yield meaningful evidence. If gains are small or difficult to observe, that also means you will have to use larger samples or repeated measurements.

Statistical significance isn't always enough, however. Here's another example of unconvincing evidence:

Example 11   Improving Children's Self-Concepts

You have a program to improve children's self-concepts. Fifteen students in a school were selected at random for the innovative program, and the remaining sixteen comprise a control group.

At the end of the six-month program you have all 31 students complete the Smith Self-Concept Inventory, which reports scores on a scale of 1 = very low to 50 = very high. The control group's average posttest score was 15 points, and the experimental group's was 17.9 points.

The difference is statistically significant, but the results probably wouldn't convince the JDRP. Why not? Because you used a small sample and you didn't repeat the experiment.

To make a more persuasive case you might repeat the same experiment in five different schools concurrently, or you might repeat it in the same school each year for three years.

Was the Effect Programmatically Significant?

A programmatically significant effect is one that is not trivial in magnitude, one that occurs in an important area, and one that can be achieved at reasonable cost. A small gain has a better chance of being considered significant if it is in a broad or important area or if it doesn't cost too much.

Programmatic significance, unlike statistical significance, is not only a technical question but a matter of judgment. Programmatic significance is sometimes established on the basis of past experience, sometimes on expert review, sometimes on theory or statistical rules of thumb.

If you use past experience, you rely on the results of previous programs. If you use expert review, you probably ask specialists to assess the project's accomplishments. A statistical rule of thumb usually links programmatic meaning to statistical significance, sometimes equating the two.

Consider the following example.

Example 12   The Health Hazards of Smoking

In order to evaluate a program designed to teach adolescents about the health hazards of smoking, you selected 510 students at random from two high schools. The remaining 511 students served as a control.

When you compared the two groups, you found that 10% more of the students in the experimental program than in the control group said they would never start smoking. The difference was statistically significant, but the program cost more than $350 for each student who participated.

If experts say that smoking is not a major health problem for adolescents, or if the results of similar programs don't hold up over time, the high cost of your project makes the gains unimpressive. If you could get the same results for $35 per student instead of $350, the intervention would stand a better chance of being judged programmatically significant.

Can the Intervention Be Implemented in Another Location with a Reasonable Expectation of Comparable Impact?

An intervention that worked once may not turn out as well when someone else tries it in another place with a different cast of characters. It might not even turn out as well tried again in the same setting with the same people. To judge the likelihood of reproducing the project with reasonable success, the JDRP considers several issues.

You should be able to show that your success isn't the result of unusual opportunities that aren't available to others. If your health center has five skilled nursing facilities nearby, you can probably do a better job of training nurses for geriatric patients than another health center without such facilities. Would your program work for them?

Second, you should be able to show that your staff isn't unique. If only one nurse trainer has used the geriatric program, it's hard to tell how much of your success can be credited to the program and how much to good leadership. The same is true even if the same trainer has repeated the program successfully several times.

Third, the JDRP wants something to show that the intervention can probably be duplicated. Most evaluations don't pay much attention to proving whether a program might be useful to others under different circumstances, but there are some ways to establish generalizability and these methods often strengthen the evaluation design.

One way to do this is to try out the program in more than one setting. It is also better to select the staff at random instead of using volunteers or those who have special training. Of course, random selection of program participants helps, too. But be careful how you interpret evaluation findings—remember that an effective sex education program for boys may not be successful with girls. If you can't show that your program works in more than one place, you can probably show that staff, facilities, and participants similar to yours exist in other places. Finally, decide which components of your program are absolutely essential and concentrate your efforts on showing that those components can be duplicated elsewhere.

How Likely Is It that the Observed Effect Resulted from the Intervention?

You can always find a number of other explanations for changes that appear to be a result of your program. Students in a nutrition project might have grown and changed even without your efforts, for example. Some may have been in another health program that helped them more than yours did.

If you don't use rigorous experimental designs, alternative explanations become especially important. Since the JDRP requires evidence that improvement is a result of your particular intervention, it's up to you to rule out the possibility that other factors were actually responsible.

Some of the factors that can be confused with program performance are history, maturation, statistical regression, mortality, instrumentation, testing, selection, and reactive effects of testing, the Hawthorne Effect and interference from other programs (see Chapter IV).

Here's an example of ruling out alternative explanations:

Example 13   Adhering to the Speed Limit

You've been asked to evaluate a program to improve adherence to the speed limit among teenagers. Suppose you review a sample of traffic tickets given to drivers under 20 for the 12 months before and after the program began and find a 20% increase in adherence the month the program started. The increase rate was maintained thereafter, so it seems reasonable to conclude that the program was responsible for the improvements.

To further support this claim you might show that no other special program for improvement of adherence took place while the experimental one was in progress. It might also help to show that no changes were made in data collection methods or in the way the information was reported.

Is the Evidence Believable and Interpretable?

The sixth and last hurdle has to do with the general quality of the evaluation evidence you present to the JDRP.

Watch for inconsistencies in your data. Do the numbers reported in texts and tables agree? If statistical tests are used, do you give all the appropriate details? Test results should be accompanied by means, standard deviations, and other supporting data. Test instruments should measure the areas you claim to be assessing.

Here are some important tips:

- Present a complete description of the evaluation's methodology and findings.

- Describe instruments in detail. Document reliability and validity information, the number of people tested, the testing dates, and the forms of the test used.

- Present data for all of the measures administered. Give types of scores (e.g., norms or raw scores). Clearly identify statistical tests and provide sample sizes each time scores are reported.

- Be sure the inferences you draw from analyses are consistent with the evaluation design and information.

- Be objective in your presentation and always describe any limitations on the evaluation's design.

HOW TO PLAN AN EVALUATION
YOU'LL BE PROUD OF

Whether you're conducting an evaluation or trying to make sense of someone else's, you probably need help deciding the critical elements that make a truly professional job.

Here, we offer a set of evaluation guidelines drawn from our own studies and experience. Follow them and you will end up with information that accurately describes what your program is, what it does, and how well it does it. You can use these guidelines to design your own evaluations or to judge the credibility of evaluations done by others.

Guideline 1: An evaluation must ask specific questions or test hypotheses about a program. Always state the evaluation questions or hypotheses in advance. This will limit the scope of the evaluation and help people understand what kind of information they can expect to get and what kind they cannot expect to get.

Here are some typical evaluation questions:

- How cohesive and visible is the program?
- How well did the program achieve its goals?
- Were the program's activities implemented as planned?
- How effective were the activities in achieving the goals?
- For which groups was the program most/least successful?
- How did social and political factors influence the program's development and impact?
- What social and political effects did the program have?
- What did the program cost?
- How well was the program managed?
- What are the merits of the program compared with alternative programs?

Example 14   Living Healthfully

Living Healthfully is a curriculum designed to make adolescents aware of common health hazards and how to avoid them. Special emphasis is placed on the effects of diet, smoking, and alcohol. A national evaluation of the program asked the following questions:

(1) How satisfied are teachers with *Living Healthfully*?
(2) Compared to students in the control program, do students who participate in *Living Healthfully* have better health habits relating to diet, smoking, and alcohol?
(3) Do students feel more able to control their health after participating in *Living Healthfully* than they did before?
(4) What is the per-classroom cost of *Living Healthfully* compared to other major health curriculums?

Guideline 2: Limit evaluation questions to those that will provide useful information for the people who expect to act on it. The evaluator may help to formulate and clarify the evaluation questions, but the final choice of questions should be left to those who will use the data.

Example 15   Suicide Hotline Evaluation

The Suicide Hotline planned an evaluation that included ten questions. The evaluator pointed out that there wasn't enough time and money to answer all ten and helped the staff narrow their questions to seven. Among the questions the staff discarded was one that asked about the cost of the program compared to similar programs. Although the evaluator suggested that another question be eliminated instead, the staff did not agree and the cost question was not included in the final selection.

Guideline 3: Every evaluation should ask questions about outcomes. Programs are designed to achieve certain purposes or objectives, and an evaluation must determine the extent to which these have been met. It should also identify any unintended effects. Questions about process are important primarily because they illuminate the reasons for certain outcomes.

Example 16   Evaluating the Half-Way House

The staff of the Half-Way House wanted to ask questions about the number of people served, their characteristics (e.g., ethnicity, sex, age), and how long they stayed in the program. The evaluator pointed out that answers to these questions alone wouldn't tell whether the program met its goal, which was to help former convicts live more productively in society.

Guideline 4: Evaluations of large-scale programs should always ask questions about costs and generalizability. Large programs are usually costly and can affect the lives of many people. It's important to know how much it cost to produce any observed results, and whether the program can be reproduced in other places. Although evaluators of smaller programs may ask the same kinds of questions, they aren't necessarily interested in whether or not the program can be duplicated.

Example 17   The Divorced Parents' Counseling Program

Sponsors of the Divorced Parents' Counseling Program wanted to show that it was worthy of adoption nationwide. They commissioned an evaluation to find out how many separated families followed their social contract for at least three years after the program and how many decided to share joint legal and physical custody of their children. The evaluation contractors suggested additional questions about how much the program cost for each participant and how much it cost for each successful family unit. They also suggested questions about the characteristics (age, sex, profession) of those who benefited most, so that they could report the conditions under which the program might be duplicated most successfully. The staff agreed that these questions were important, and they were included in the evaluation.

Guideline 5: Standards of program merit should be set for each evaluation question. Standards are your criteria for making judgments about how well the program is working. They may be stated in terms of levels of success, comparisons among groups, and changes over time.

Example 18   The Judicial Library Reference Search

The evaluation of the Judicial Library Reference Search (JLRS) project asked "How satisfied are users of JLRS with the service they received?"

The standards set for interpreting the information collected are stated in terms of levels of success: At least 80% of the users will indicate that

(1) information given to them on the phone was helpful and easy to understand;
(2) the person who handled their inquiry was courteous and well in-formed;
(3) all their questions were answered;
(4) additional information promised was received and useful; and
(5) they took some action as a result of help from JLRS.

The JLRS evaluation also asked "Does the JLRS training program give volunteers the skills and knowledge needed to assist users?"

The standards set for this question are based on changes over time. At the end of their training

(1) trainees will show mastery of 75% of the legal library skills con-sidered important by their trainers;
(2) trainees will answer the phone and complete the phone logs with 80% accuracy;
(3) at least 80% of the trainees will feel prepared to assist users; and
(4) no more than 20% of the trainees will be dissatisfied with the scope, content, or pacing of the training they received.

Guideline 6: Standards of merit must be set before any data collection begins. Once you begin collecting data it's easy to be influenced by what you've learned. If most participants like the program, you may overlook other important aspects of the evaluation. Another reason for setting standards in advance is to help you select the evaluation design, sampling methods, instruments, and data analysis techniques that will produce the information needed to answer the questions and compare with the standards.

Example 19   The Teacher In-Service Training Seminar

The evaluation of the Teacher In-Service Training Seminar asked whether the participants were satisfied with the program. The evaluators surveyed the participants without establishing any criterion for satisfaction. The survey data showed that 80% were satisfied with the program. The client was content with these results, and the evaluators therefore decided that the answer to the evaluation question was yes. An external reviewer charged that the findings influenced the client, and asked what would have happened if only 75% of the respondents had been satisfied.

Guideline 7: Evaluation standards must have scientific validity. Standards with scientific validity can be based on expert judgment, past experience and empirical data. Empirical data come from experimental designs in which one or more groups are systematically selected and observed over time.

Statistically significant differences over time or across groups are not synonymous with scientifically valid standards. Statistical findings are valid only when viewed along with program standards. A statistically significant outcome is one that is unlikely to occur by chance, and a significant program outcome is one that makes a meaningful difference in meeting program goals.

Statistical significance is usually determined as part of the data analysis process; it is not necessarily the same as programmatic significance. When you have a large number of people, it is possible to observe statistically significant outcomes that do not represent real gains in performance or any other changes that are truly important.

Example 20   A Clinical Pharmacy Program

An evaluation of a clinical pharmacy program in a hospital asked "How satisfied are users with the Drug Information Service?" The standard of satisfaction set for this question was that at least 80% of users should indicate satisfaction with the service. The choice of 80% was based on a study (Fink and Kosecoff, 1978) that found that, on the average, two out of ten people can be expected to state some dissatisfaction with educational activities or services, and that a level of dissatisfaction of 25% or less is associated with repeated use of an educational program.

Another evaluation question was: "Is good quality of care being provided?" The evaluator, the program staff, and the hospital administration agreed that the ultimate standard of good quality medical and pharmacy care is that patient outcomes improve. Since a study that focused on outcomes was beyond the scope of the evaluation, the standard that was set for answering the question was that, compared with a control group, the process of pharmaceutical care used by clinical pharmacists conformed more closely to criteria known to be associated with beneficial patient outcomes. Specifically, six drugs were selected because of their prevalence and potential for abuse: carbenicillin, methyldopa, nafcillin, phenytoin, digoxin, and procainamide. The process criteria covered such concerns as:

- patients with a history of allergy to a given drug not being dosed with the drug,
- 90% of patients being dosed properly initially,
- all patients being dosed properly within a given number of days/ hours,
- adverse drug reactions being promptly identified and patients taken off the drug,
- patients being taken off a drug once they no longer need it, and
- dosage being appropriately adjusted or new drug therapy being initiated when patients do not respond to a drug.

Guideline 8: Select a design suited to each evaluation question. Each evaluation question may use different independent and dependent variables and different standards. Choose a design that respects these differences.

Each of the major designs—case, time-series, and comparison group—has certain strengths:

- *Case designs* examine a single, cohesive group. Questions about new or exemplary programs for which comparisons are not yet available almost always require case designs.

- *Time-series designs* compare a group's current performance with its past performance. Time series are useful in measuring how lasting a program's effects are.

- *Comparison group design* measures the performance of an experimental group by comparing it to the performance of a control group. For the design to be true experimental rather than quasi-experimental, the comparison groups must be selected so that they are equivalent at the beginning of the evaluation.

Each design has features that guard against certain biases. True experimental design is the most trustworthy.

The evaluator should be confident that his or her design ensures maximum internal validity (that is, observed changes are due to the program and not to outside events). Not all biases affecting validity are equally likely in a given situation, nor are all evaluation questions equally important.

Example 21   A Teaching Hospital's Drug Information Program

The University Teaching Hospital is conducting an evaluation of a drug information program for patients in the geriatric unit. One evaluation question asks about the program's impact on participants' drug-taking behavior and knowledge. One of the standards stipulates that participants' drug-taking behavior must improve by at least one-third of a standard deviation over a three-month period, and then sustain itself for at least six months. To answer the evaluation question, a time-series design is being used in which participants are measured every three months, beginning six months before the program and continuing for one year thereafter. The evaluator is aware of the following possible threats to the design's internal validity:

- *history* (some concurrent, but external, factor such as the Gray Panther movement might change participants' awareness of their drug behavior and its consequences)

- *maturation* (participants' knowledge and actions may change naturally over time)

- *testing* (participants may remember the answers they gave to various evaluation instruments and repeat them from time to time)

- *instrumentation* (there may be changes in the way instruments are administered from time to time)

- *mortality* (in an elderly population many participants may die or lose their ability to care for themselves)

The evaluator has decided, however, that external factors such as history and maturation would probably not alter significantly the participants' behavior; testing and mortality, however, are considered potentially important threats. The time-series design is being used anyway because it allows participants to act as their own controls and is considered to be responsive to the evaluation question.

Example 22   ESL Classes

The State Department of Education commissioned an evaluation of its English-as-a-second-language classes for the public. One of the evaluation questions asked how satisfied participants were with the program. An 80% satisfaction rate was set as the standard, based on the experience of several similar programs.

The evaluator chose a case design in which all participants were asked to complete a 10-item questionnaire at the conclusion of the classes. The evaluator decided that history, maturation, and instrumentation were unlikely to be problems, although mortality might be. (Testing and selection were not pertinent to this design.) The evaluator therefore accepted the case design as probably adequate for the evaluation question.

Guideline 9: For evaluation questions dealing with important issues or large-scale studies, use a design that establishes causality. A good evaluation design controls many if not all of the likely threats to internal validity. However, this control alone does not ensure that the program causes the observed changes. The only way to establish causality is with a true experimental design that compares two or more programs and assigns subjects randomly to treatment or placebo groups. The next best alternative to the true experimental design is the quasi-experimental design, in which the groups that are compared are very similar, though not technically equivalent. Scientific proof of a program's merit is especially important when large sums of money or many people are involved or when a program is controversial.

Example 23   Disease and Personality Type

The Center for New Healing held that many diseases resulted from unconscious or conscious conflicts associated with certain personality types. In addition to traditional medical treatments, patients at the center could get intensive psychotherapy. To test the value of their program, the center created a demonstration project for patients between 30 and 55 years of age with newly diagnosed depression. The evaluation standards required that at least 60% of the patients remain symptom free one year after their diagnosis for the program to be considered successful.

The evaluator first considered a time-series design, with patients monitored every other month for one year. Although the design was compatible with the evaluation question and its standards, an expert panel argued that because the program was controversial, better evidence was needed to prove it was the program that was responsible for the absence of symptoms. A 60% symptom-free rate, though better than most predictions, could conceivably appear without any special program. Guided by the panel's advice, the evaluator randomly assigned subjects to a conventional drug therapy group or to a group that combined conventional care and psychotherapy and monitored both groups for twelve months.

Guideline 10: For each question, select a sample representative of the population to which the findings will be applied. In evaluating national programs, use samples that reflect the nation's population in terms of geography, sex, age, ethnicity, socioeconomic status, and so on. In evaluating relatively restricted programs, use samples that reflect the composition of that specific population.

Example 24   The Alcohol Awareness Hotline

One question in a statewide evaluation of the Alcohol Awareness Hotline was whether people knew more about alcoholism after the hotline was established. The standard required a statistically significant gain of one-fifth of a standard deviation over two years for the program to be considered successful.

The evaluator used a time-series design in which a sample of citizens was interviewed in June 1979 and in June 1980. The sample was selected to be representative of the state's population. Using census data, the evaluator divided the state according to geographic areas, urban and rural populations, and high- and low-income groups. A random stratified sample was then drawn.

Guideline 11: Sample size should be determined by the extent of the effect that is considered to be meaningful. For important or controversial evaluation questions, large samples are needed if policymakers are to be convinced that the findings are trustworthy. Also, a large sample is helpful in detecting unanticipated, but significant, program consequences. Given the size of the effect that is considered meaningful (which should be stipulated by the standards) and an estimate of the standard deviation for the dependent variable in the population (which can be obtained from previous studies or pretesting), it is possible to compute a sample size that is adequate to detect, with statistical precision, the desired changes.

It is not always possible, however, to obtain a sample size large enough to be convincing. To compensate for small samples, the evaluator can repeat observations several times with different (but equivalent) samples. Repetition with different samples can provide supporting data for the generalizations of a program's effects: repetition with equivalent samples supports statements about the reliability of a program's outcomes.

Example 25   Evaluation and the Martial Arts

The First School District was evaluating its five-week martial arts program for parents, teachers, and students. One of the evaluation questions was whether the new program worked better than the old program.

The evaluator used a true experimental comparison group design. Each week new participants were assigned at random to the new or old groups. After twelve weeks in the program, participants were tested using a specially designed performance measure. The test was scored on a scale from 0 to 10. The evaluation standards stipulated that a one-tenth of a point difference must be observed between the two groups. The standard deviation in the population ($SD_{x1 - x2}$) was .788 in studies with similar populations. Using this statistic and a one-tenth of a point difference ($\bar{X}_1 - \bar{X}_2 = 0.1$), the evaluator calculated a sample size of 626 for each group.

To obtain a sample of 1252 (two groups of 626), the evaluator estimated that all people new to the program over a period of 34 weeks must be included in the study, with individuals randomly assigned to groups at the end of each week. The evaluator estimated that 56 people would start the program each week and 83% would meet the criterion of being willing to remain in the program five weeks. Even with this commitment, the evaluator assumed a 20% dropout rate:

56 participants each week

83% eligible = .83 × 56 = .4648

80% likely to remain in study = .80 × .4648 = .3718

The evaluator could expect 37 participants each week, or 1258 participants in 34 weeks.

Guideline 12: Use instruments that are reliable, valid, and suited to the evaluation question. Data collection techniques should provide consistent and accurate information. Most standardized instruments have been pilot tested and are usually reliable. If, however, the evaluator has created a new instrument, or if the statistics on the standardized measure are from an inappropriate sample, then systematic pilot testing and validation are necessary.

Instruments should be specifically designed to obtain the information called for by an evaluation question. Collecting extraneous information is costly and bothersome to the respondent, and it obscures the real focus of the evaluation.

Example 26   The Pediatric Psychosocial Support Unit

One question for an evaluation of the Pediatric Psychosocial Support Unit asked whether the program helped children adjust to school after they left the hospital. The evaluator found three possible tests to measure adjustment. The first, the Beck Adjustment to School Inventory, had high content validity, asked only pertinent questions, and was easy to administer and interpret. Unfortunately, no reliability and validity statistics were available. The second, the Rappaport School Assessment Scale, had been validated only on a population of healthy children. The third test, the Grosse Attitude to School Test, was longer and more costly than the others.

The evaluator chose the Grosse test, despite its drawbacks, because it had been validated on both healthy populations and special populations (including handicapped and chronically ill children) and had higher test/retest reliability statistics for healthy children than did the Rappaport Scale.

Guideline 13: Use more than one method of collecting information when assessing important issues. The instruments used in an evaluation can always be challenged. One person may complain that a particular test doesn't measure something he or she considers important; another might not like the test's format; still another might argue that unless the test has perfect validity, it cannot be credible. Therefore, when dealing with important issues, use more than one instrument or technique for collecting the same information.

You should use professionally developed instruments to assess interests, values, attitudes, or psychological states. Unfortunately, these instruments are not always available. In such instances, rely on two or more different instruments that, taken together, provide more convincing data than would any single measure.

Example 27   Costs of the Gifted Students Program

The most controversial question raised by the Gifted Students Program concerned the per-student costs. The evaluator used the Newhouse Marginal Costs audit procedure, a true experimental design that compared the costs per student in a variety of programs. This procedure had been used reliably in similar programs, but the evaluator noted that some economists had claimed the procedure was too innovative. The evaluator therefore decided to also use a second, very conservative technique to provide supporting data.

Guideline 14: Keep data collection as unobtrusive as possible. In collecting data, the evaluator should avoid using people's time and talents when other alternatives are possible. Data collection should not needlessly infringe upon people's privacy. Obey privacy laws.

Example 28   Senior Citizens and a
Community Center

An evaluation question asked which senior citizens made most use of a community center's facilities. The evaluator proposed a case design that required interviews. The center's administrators considered the interviews too much of a burden on members and suggested that the evaluator get the information from the center's records or observations.

Guideline 15: Use analysis techniques that are technically sound and suited to the quality of the data. Information collection usually produces data of varying quality. Sometimes instruments of questionable validity are used; at other times good instruments are used incorrectly. Sophisticated and costly analytic techniques are often wasted on questionable data. Remember, sound technique and reliable data go hand in hand.

Example 29   Parent-Child Interaction

The evaluation of the Parent-Child Interaction Workshop asked if parents had changed their opinions about the role of listening in fostering better relationships. The evaluation standards required a statistically significant change of 2 points on a 20-point evaluation scale administered at the beginning of the program and at its conclusion.

The evaluator planned to use repeated measures analysis of variance for data from this time-series design. Unfortunately, the person hired to make the surveys produced a response rate of 30 out of a possible 130 at the beginning of the program and 122 out of 130 at its end. The evaluator had to abandon the time-series design and repeated measures analysis in favor of a case design and descriptive statistics.

Guideline 16: Interpret analysis results in terms of the evaluation questions and standards. An evaluation will typically provide a great deal of information, not all of which is relevant to every question. Do not interpret results as a whole, but in terms of each question and its associated standards. Do not extrapolate beyond the limits of the analysis results.

Example 30   Continuing Education and Retirement Plans

An evaluation question asked "Are employers satisfied with their continuing education program or retirement plans?" The standards stipulated that at least 80% of the respondents state that the program met their needs and that what they learned could be of use in their work.

The evaluator used a case design in which each participating employer filled out a questionnaire at the end of the program. A descriptive statistics analysis showed that 89% felt the program met their needs, and 75% found the information useful in their work. The evaluator reported these data and concluded that because the standards had not been met, the answer to the evaluation question was no.

Guideline 17: Report techniques and results so they are meaningful to both the layperson and the professional. It is an evaluator's responsibility to communicate clearly what was done, how it was done, and why it was done. A statistician should be able to follow the analytic discussion without feeling the need to question the logic or fill in the details. Others should be able to understand your methods and results without consulting a statistician. If necessary, provide summaries of technical data.

Example 31   PSRO 122

PSRO 122, as part of its medical care evaluation obligations, funded an educational program on the use of adriamycin to treat breast and bowel cancer patients. One of the questions asked in the program evaluation was "Has there been a statistically and educationally significant increase in physicians' knowledge about treatment of cancer with adriamycin?"

The evaluators tested the participating physicians one month before and three months after the program. The 20-item Cancer Therapy Test (CTT) had been shown to have test/retest reliability of .91 and validities of .80 to .89. The standard required one-half of a standard deviation gain in physicians' knowledge for the program to be judged successful. The evaluator collected data from 126 physicians, conducting a dependent t test to determine whether their knowledge about adriamycin treatment had increased. The independent variable for the analysis was time of testing, pre-, and postinstruction. The dependent variable was physicians' knowledge as represented by their CTT scores. The hypotheses tested in the analysis were as follows:

Null Hypothesis: Pretest mean score = Posttest mean score
Alternative Hypothesis: Pretest mean score < Posttest mean score

The evaluator tabulated the results as follows:

	Preinstruction	Postinstruction
Mean*	9.25	14.72
SD	4.32	4.26
N	126	126
Correlation	.75	.75
t value	20.38	20.38
df	125	125
significance (1-tailed)	.01	.01

*Total possible score on CTT = 20 points.

The table shows that the t value is significant, indicating that the increase in the physicians' knowledge was statistically meaningful. The 5.47 point increase from pre- to posttest was also educationally meaningful since it exceeded the criterion of a half a standard deviation gain.

Guideline 18: An evaluation report should answer the evaluation questions and explain how each was arrived at. The evaluation report is the official public record of the evaluation. If interested people don't have access to the report or don't understand the report, then the evaluator has failed to fulfill a major responsibility.

A good report clearly and logically describes each evaluation question and the procedures used to get each answer. The report should include:

- an introduction to the evaluation, the evaluation questions, the evaluation standards, and the limitations on the scope of the evaluation;
- the design strategy and sampling procedures for each evaluation question and the limitations on internal and external validity;
- the information collection techniques and instruments and the limitations on their reliability and validity;
- the methods used to analyze the evaluation information, the limitations of each method, and the results of each analysis;
- the answer to each evaluation question, including interpretation of findings and recommendations; and
- administrative details such as schedules and staff assignments.

Guideline 19: Offer recommendations only on those aspects of a program that the evaluation is specifically designed to study—and then only if asked to do so. Recommendations technically are not a part of an evaluation study because they do not provide data. Sometimes, however, the evaluator is asked to make recommendations. In such a case suggest how to improve or certify the effectiveness of a program. Avoid recommending whether a program be funded or discontinued. Funding decisions often involve political considerations that an evaluator may not be fully aware of.

Example 32   Program Costs and Staff Attitudes

An evaluation examined the relative merits of programs X, Y, and Z in terms of total program costs and staff attitudes. Staff attitudes were reported on a 5-point scale, with 5 being good and 1 being poor. Yearly costs per patient were reported for each program.

The data analysis found that program X, with 11 staff and 200 patients, was the most economical ($310 per patient per year), followed by program Y, with 15 staff and 200 patients ($352 per patient), and program Z, with 18 staff and 247 patients ($409 per patient). Staff attitudes were best in program Z (4.2), followed by program Y (3.2), and program X (2.1).

When asked to make recommendations, the evaluator pointed out that the poor attitudes of the staff in program X could be related to the program's relatively small size and recommended an investigation of this possibility.

CHAPTER

Setting Standards

ALL EVALUATIONS ARE CONCERNED WITH providing information about program merit. Among the questions evaluation studies ask are: How effective is the program? Is it worth the effort and expense? Have all its influences been beneficial? How well off would we have been if there had been no program? Of necessity, then, evaluations are studies that result in judgments of quality. Unfortunately, there are no generally agreed upon definitions of quality, and therein lies one of the evaluator's greatest challenges: How to design a study whose appraisals are considered objective and fair.

In this chapter, we provide some guidelines for making judgments of merit. In the first section, four ways of setting standards of program quality are offered. All four rely on the support of the evaluator's sponsors for approval and to help ensure that criteria have been set, to the extent possible, without bias. The Evaluator's Program Description is also described as a vehicle for finding out what the evaluation sponsor and consumer want to know and will accept as evidence of program merit. In the second section we describe two models for setting minimum standards of competency whenever achievement is to be measured.

HOW TO SET EVALUATION STANDARDS

Setting evaluation standards means deciding what kind of information will provide convincing evidence of a program's success. A

65

program is usually considered successful if it meets its goals, if the activities it uses to achieve those goals are beneficial, and if any unexpected effects of the program are positive.

Actual evidence that a program has merit can be in the form of statements, events, objects, and observations that testify to its quality. In a continuing education program to improve counseling skills in working with alcoholics, for example, evidence of merit might include any or all of the following:

- a measured gain in counselors' skills (based on a paper-and-pencil test)

- an observed gain in counselors' skills (based on performance tests or observation rating scales)

- testimony from couselors that their skills have improved (based on questionnaire or interview information)

- testimony from clients that counselors appear to have improved their skills (based on questionnaire or interview information)

- a measured gain in mental health of alcoholics (based on psychological tests)

- a measured gain in numbers of alcoholics who comfortably avoid drinking over a specified period of time (based on observations and surveys)

Reaching agreement about what constitutes evidence of a program's merit is one of the most difficult aspects of planning an evaluation. Don't look for generally accepted guidelines to help you answer questions such as "How much learning must take place for a continuing medical education program to be considered educationally meaningful?" or "How effective is the XYZ Behavior Modification Program in assisting obese patients to adhere to their diets?" There aren't any guidelines. There are, however, at least four methods you can use to set evaluation standards.

Experts

First, you can call on experts to set standards. Take, for example, a program to improve science education in county schools in the most cost-effective way. You might ask chemists, biochemists, and other scientists to define what constitutes a sufficient education in science for high school students for the program to be considered effective. Similarly, you could ask businesspersons and economists to set standards for evaluating the program's financial efficiency.

Expert judgment is sometimes the best way (and occasionally the only way) to arrive at realistic standards for new or innovative programs, and it is an efficient way to set standards when general consensus can be reached. You run the risk of having criteria that reflect the biases of the experts, rather than the realities of the program, however.

Past Performance

A second method you can use to set standards is to rely on past performance to determine reasonable expectations. Sometimes you can obtain standards by using statistical techniques such as regression analysis that provide estimates of adequate performance based on people's past performance or the performance of other similar individuals.

Standards derived from reasonable expectations have the advantage of being based on experience, but they have the disadvantage of assuming that the past will duplicate the present in a predictable way or that past performance is acceptable.

Comparisons

A third method of setting evaluation standards relies on comparisons. Comparisons can be made of one group's performance over time, among several groups' performances at one time, or among several groups over time. Standards based on comparisons are relatively easy to understand and measure, but it is sometimes difficult to decide how large differences must be for them to be meaningful. When interpreting differences, programmatic and statistical significance are sometimes confused. A statistically significant difference is one that is unlikely to occur by chance; a programmatically significant difference is one that is meaningful in terms of a program's goals.

Statistical significance is usually determined as part of the data analysis process. It is not necessarily synonymous with programmatic significance. With very large numbers of people, it is possible to obtain statistically significant outcomes that do not really represent gains in performance or changes in attitudes or behaviors that are important or meaningful results of a program.

Suppose students in new Language Arts Program A read, on the average, five more books than students in Program B, for example. Someone will have to decide whether the difference is of sufficient magnitude to justify the development, implementation, and costs of Program A. Is the increase actually worth the investment?

Norms

Relying on established practice or norms is the fourth method of setting standards. For example, standards for achievement can be based on performing at the 50th percentile or better.

Comparisons with established practice provide easily understood evidence of program merit, but they sometimes overlook regional variations in needs, costs and resources. There is also the possibility that the standards are not meaningful for a particular program. And sometimes normative data just don't exist.

To make sure your evaluation is credible, get together with whoever is sponsoring the evaluation to decide what kind of information it takes to prove that the program is worthwhile. Establishing evaluation standards is extremely important because it helps you identify the information the evaluation must produce, and it forces your client (the evaluation sponsor) to be truthful and realistic about what the program is really expected to achieve. It protects the evaluator against claims that the findings are not relevant or sufficient to prove the program's success or failure, and it protects the sponsor against having the evaluator arbitrarily collect information claimed to be "good" or "important."

The Evaluator's Program Description

To help you understand a program's goals and activities and learn what will be accepted as convincing evidence of success, we use a form called the Evaluator's Program Description (EPD). The EPD is a convenient way to record information about goals and activities along with the evidence needed to prove that each goal has been achieved and that each activity has taken place as planned. We have field tested the EPD in large and small evaluations and we know it works. Example 33 provides an outline of an Evaluator's Program Description.

EXAMPLE 33   An Evaluator's Program Description

Goals	Activities	Evidence of Program Merit
One by one, describe the goals each program is aiming to achieve.	For each goal, describe the activities that are expected to lead to fulfillment of the goal.	For each goal and activity, describe the type of information that will be convincing evidence of program merit.

Step 1: How to record goals and activities. A program goal is a statement of intent. An activity is a means of achieving a goal. In completing the EPD, you should describe one or more of the activities that are planned to help meet each goal. For example, the goals and activities columns of an EPD might look like those in Example 34.

Many programs don't have precisely stated goals, and the relationship between their goals and activities is unclear. You may have to persuade the program staff to rephrase the goals and activities more clearly, or you may decide to rely on your own experience and logic to come up with them. In some cases, however, even when the goals and activities have been identified and the relationships among them have been established, you will still find yourself faced with a list of intentions that are too vague for evaluation purposes.

Step 2: How to determine evidence of program merit. When you meet with the evaluation sponsors, ask them this question: What would it take to convince you that this is a successful program? Summarize the answers to this question in the third column of the EPD. List at least one indication of program merit for each goal and activity you're evaluating. Example 35 lists several kinds of evidence that might be acceptable for the pharmacy program already mentioned.

Notice that although the two goals for the program were not stated behaviorally, the evidence of program merit describes exactly what students must be able to do or know and exactly what activities must take place if the program is to be judged a success.

The precision demanded in arriving at evidence of program merit actually operationalizes the goals, that is, it makes them measurable. It also highlights the particular program activities that are of special inter-

Example 34   A Partially Completed EPD for a Program for Pharmacy Students

Goals	Activities	Evidence of Program Merit
1. To make pharmacists knowledgeable about drugs' effects.	Pharmacy students observe human reactions to drugs. Pharmacy students attend lectures on the nature and treatment of frequently occurring problems.	
2. To teach students how to conduct drug audits using medical charts.	Students learn how to read medical charts. Students conduct supervised chart audits in nursing homes.	

est for the evaluation. This system permits you to leave the program's original goals and activities intact. It means the program developers don't ever have to restate them completely for the purpose of the evaluation.

Where to find information for the EPD. To complete the Evaluator's Program Description, you may need to consult the program sponsors, staff and documents, the evaluation sponsors and others affected by the evaluation.

Written documents are among the most useful, easily obtained, and least expensive sources of information for evaluating a program that is still developing. These documents include the project proposal, earlier evaluation reports, and products or materials developed by the program or for use in the program.

To be sure you understand the program well enough to describe accurately its goals and activities, it's crucial to consult with the people who created and implemented it. No matter how old the program is, it's always a good idea to enlist the help of program staff. They can provide valuable insight, and involving them in planning the evaluation may make it easier to obtain their cooperation for later activities.

Example 35   A Completed EPD for a Program for Pharmacy Students

Goals	Activities	Evidence of Program Merit
To make pharmacists knowledgeable about drugs' effects.	Pharmacy students observe human reactions to drugs. Pharmacy students attend lectures on the nature and treatment of frequently occurring problems.	A statistically significant improvement in student performance from the beginning to the end of the program. Documentation that students attended lectures on the nature and treatment of frequently occurring problems.
To teach students how to conduct drug audits using medical charts.	Students learn how to read medical charts. Students conduct supervised chart audits in nursing homes.	Supervisors rate students' drug audits as satisfactory.

Don't forget to include the program's sponsors in preparing the EPD. They provide financial support for the program, and their help can make the evaluation run more efficiently and lend credibility to its findings. Other people you may want to talk to include the program participants and their families, advisory committees, and other citizen's groups. They can give you valuable information about the political and social atmosphere in which the program was created and currently exists.

Be sure to take a preliminary draft of the EPD to your client (whoever commissioned the evaluation) for review and amendments. Depending on the nature, purpose, and size of the program, this document will undergo many changes before it satisfies everyone. Sometimes it's enough for you to meet individually with the program director or evaluation sponsor to produce a description of the program that is adequate for evaluation purposes. In other cases, you may be involved in a long series of meetings, starting with the program director and eventually including the program's staff and advisory committee, members of the local community, and even people from the funding agency.

The number of meetings and drafts of the EPD will vary, but the basic process is the same each time: The evaluator meets with a group of people to review and critique the most recent draft of the EPD and then updates the EPD on the basis of their comments. Review meetings may be formal or informal and often the meeting will be no more than a phone call or a brief note.

Once you have a complete description of the program's goals, activities, and evidence of merit, and your client has accepted that description as the basis for the evaluation, then the EPD is complete. Make sure that the final version of the EPD is available to everyone who participated in its development.

Step 3: How to formulate the right evaluation questions. After you have completed the Evaluator's Program Description, you are ready to decide what questions the evaluation should answer. The evaluation questions are the heart of the evaluation, and all activities must be organized so that they can be answered efficiently.

One of the best places to turn for the evaluation questions is the program merit column of the EPD, because there you will find definitions of successful accomplishment of goals and activities. You can easily transform this information into questions about how well the goals were achieved and how successful the activities were.

Example 36   A Pharmacy Program

If the evidence of program merit column says: (1) pharmacy students who participate in the program perform significantly better than students who do not, and (2) supervisors give pharmacy students satisfactory evaluations . . . then consider these evaluation questions:

(1) Did pharmacy students who participated in the program perform significantly better than students who did not?
(2) Did supervisors evaluate students' drug audits as being satisfactory?

For many evaluations, particularly those with small budgets, all evaluation questions can be drawn directly from the EPD. Larger evaluations may call for answers to additional questions.

Remember that the evaluation questions are not the evaluator's questions. They are asked by those who commissioned the evaluation and who must use the evaluation information. Sometimes you'll have no trouble working together to arrive at evaluation questions. Sometimes the questions may have been chosen long before the evaluation, at the time of program planning. In this case you should check to be sure that your client still accepts those questions as important and no new ones need to be added. Occasionally the evaluation questions are mandated by law—you may add to them but you can't substitute one for another or omit any of the mandated questions.

HOW TO SET MINIMUM COMPETENCY LEVELS OF PERFORMANCE

The notion of competencies or minimum levels of performance has been a concern of evaluators for some time. Robert Ebel and Leo Nedelsky have developed two different models for arriving at minimum standards that are relatively easy to adapt.

Nedelsky's Model

Step 1: Have instructors review each test item. In Nedelsky's model, two or more instructors should review each item on a test using the following directions:

> On each item of the test, cross out those responses that the lowest D student should be able to reject as incorrect. To the left of the item, write the reciprocal of the number of remaining responses. Thus, if you cross out one of five responses, write one quarter ($\frac{1}{4}$).

Example 37   Light Waves

Light has wave characteristics. Which of the following is the best experimental evidence of this statement?

    (A) Light can be reflected by a mirror.

    (B) Light forms dark and light bands on passing through a small opening.

    (C) A beam of white light can be broken into its component colors by a prism.

    (D) Light carries energy.

$\frac{1}{4}$ (E) Light operates a photoelectric cell.

Step 2: Compare and discuss scoring standards. After the instructors have marked five or six items, Nedelsky says they should hold a brief conference to compare and discuss the scoring standards they used. After the conference, the instructors continue to work alone.

Step 3: Compute the minimum passing score. First you need to know Nedelsky's terminology:

- Responses that the lowest D students should be able to reject as incorrect, and that therefore should be primarily attractive to F students, are called F responses. (In the example above, response E was the only F response in the opinion of the instructor who marked the item.)

- Students who possess just enough knowledge to reject F responses are called F-D students, to suggest borderline knowledge between F and D.

- The most probable mean score of the F-D students on a test is called the F-D guess score and is denoted by M_{FD}. M_{FD} is equal (mathematically) to the sum of the reciprocals of the numbers of responses other than F responses. (In the example above, the reciprocal is $\frac{1}{4}$.)

- The most probable vlaue of the standard deviation corresponding to M_{FD} is denoted by s_{FD}. (Although the value of M_{FD} must be accurately computed for each test, s_{FD} may be given an approximate value. If, on the average, an F student will reject one out of five possible alternatives on a test item, then one estimate for s_{FD} is $.4\sqrt{N}$ where N = the number of test items.

The minimum passing score is equal to the average of the F-D guess scores obtained by various instructors, plus a constant (k) multiplied by the standard deviation of the guess scores (ks_{FD}).

$$\text{Minimum passing score} = M_{FD} + ks_{FD}$$

The k is an estimate made by the people who set the competencies and it determines how many of the F-D students (those who don't necessarily know the right answer but who manage to avoid the wrong one) will fail. Assigning to k the values –1, 0, 1, and 2 will (on the average) result in failing 16%, 50%, 84%, and 98% of the F-D students.

It is better to reach an informal decision on the value of k after the instructors choose the F responses because it is easier then to estimate the rigor of their scoring standards. Nedelsky says you should agree on the value of k before the values of M_{FD} are computed and certainly before the students' scores are known.

Example 38   Minimum Competencies in Eclectic Knowledge

Suppose Frank Jones, a high school teacher, wanted to use the following 6-item test to establish minimum competencies in eclectic knowledge. To do so, he invited three of his colleagues to use Nedelsky's model to establish a minimum passing score. The instructors met and assigned k = 1 in order to fail 84% of the F-D students. Here are the ratings of each item made by instructor 1, instructor 2, and instructor 3.

1. What changes occur in the composition of the air in a lighted airtight room in which the only things are growing plants?

Instructor:	1	2	3	
	A	A	A.	Carbon dioxide increases and oxygen decreases.
	B	B	B.	Carbon dioxide decreases and oxygen increases.
	¼C̸	¼C̸	1/3C̸.	Both carbon dioxide and oxygen increase.
	D	D	D.	Both carbon dioxide and oxygen decrease.
	E	E	E̸.	No changes occur in carbon dioxide or oxygen levels.

average reciprocal = 5/18

2. Which word is misspelled?

Instructor:	1	2	3	
	A	A	A.	Ocurred
	B	B	B.	Contrary
	C	C	C.	Symphony
	¼D	D	¼D.	Maturation
	E̸	E̸	E̸.	Weird

average reciprocal = 1/4

3. Which of the following has been responsible for the greatest changes in characteristics of domestic dogs?

Instructor:	1	2	3	
	A	A	A.	Influence of environment on heredity
	B̸	B̸	B.	Organic evolution
	C	C	C.	Selective breeding
	¼D	¼D	¼D.	Survival of the fittest
	E	E	E̸.	Increasing ozone levels

average reciprocal = 1/4

(continued)

Example 38   (Continued)

4. To whom did the title of the Broadway musical "Top Banana" refer?

Instructor: 1   2   3

A	A	A. The dictator of a Central American country.
B	B	B̸. The warden of a penitentiary.
C	C	C. The leading comedian in a burlesque theatre.
¼D	¼D	¼D. The president of a large fruit company.
E̸	E̸	E. A large yellow-haired woman named June.

average reciprocal = 1/4

5. A high protective tariff on Swiss watches in the United States is intended to most directly benefit:

Instructor: 1   2   3

A	A	A. Swiss watchmakers
B	B	B̸. United States citizens who buy Swiss watches
C	C	C. United States government officials
¼D	¼D	1/3D. United States watchmakers
E̸	E̸	E̸. Makers of Japanese watches assembled in the United States

average reciprocal = 5/18

6. What happened in 1953 to the proposed act of Congress granting statehood to Hawaii?

Instructor: 1   2   3

A	A	A. It was passed by both the House and Senate.
B	B	B. It was defeated in both the House and the Senate.
C	C	C. It was passed in the House but not by the Senate.
¼D	¼D	¼D. No act regarding statehood for Hawaii was introduced in either the House or the Senate.
E̸	E̸	E̸. It was passed in the House but then was vetoed by the president.

average reciprocal = 1/4

Using these ratings, the minimum passing score was computed to be 2.53 and Mr. Jones decided to fail any student who obtained a score of 2 or below.

$$M_{FD} = 5/18 + 1/4 + 1/4 = 1/4 + 5/18 + 1/4 = 1.55$$

$$k = 1$$

$$s_{FD} = .4\sqrt{6} = .98$$

Example 39   Illustrative Use of Ebel's Relevance and Difficulty, and Categories to Estimate Expected Success

Relevance	Difficulty		
	Easy	Medium	Hard
Essential	100%	75%	50%
Important	90%	65%	40%
Acceptable	75%	45%	30%
Questionable	50%	25%	10%

Ebel's Model

In Ebel's approach, you derive the minimum passing score from a subjective analysis of the relevance and difficulty of each item in a test. Ebel uses four categories of relevance (essential, important, acceptable and questionable) and three categories of difficulty (easy, medium and hard).

Step 1: Estimate performance of "barely passing" test taker. Suppose three experts meet to review a 100-item test and to set a minimum passing score using Ebel's method. First, they must estimate the percentage of items in each category that a barely passing examinee ought to be able to answer correctly. For example, experts or test designers may decide that for essential items, minimally qualified examinees must answer correctly 100% of all easy items, 75% of all items of medium difficulty, and 50% of all hard items (Example 39). If the relevance of the item is questionable rather than essential, qualified test takers need only answer 50% of all easy items correctly, 25% of all items of medium difficulty correctly, and 10% of all hard items correctly.

Step 2: Assign each item to a relevance and difficulty category. Next, they should independently assign each item to a relevance and difficulty category. Summarize the ratings of the three judges as in Example 40.

In reading the table in Example 40, notice that the sum of the "number of items" column is 300. This is because each of three raters assigned 100 items to the various categories of relevance and difficulty. No items are assigned to the category of essential but easy because none of the experts found any items to fit this classification.

The "expected success" column gives the percentage of examinees expected to answer items correctly in each category, as shown in the

Example 40   Computation of Minimum Passing Score

Item Category	Number of Items	% Expected Success	Number X Success
Essential			
Easy		100	
Medium	21	75	1575
Hard	53	50	2650
Important			
Easy	24	90	2160
Medium	49	65	3185
Hard	38	40	1520
Acceptable			
Easy	24	75	1800
Medium	59	45	2655
Hard	19	30	570
Questionable			
Easy	4	50	200
Medium	7	25	175
Hard	2	10	20
	300		16510

16510/300 = 55.03 or 55% = Minimum Passing Score

table in Example 39. The fourth column is the product of the values in the second and third columns.

Finally, the minimum passing score is the sum of the fourth column divided by the total number of items assigned to categories (the total of column 2). In this case, the minimum passing score is 16510/300 = 55.03% or 55%.

CHAPTER IV

Designing Evaluations and Selecting Samples

THE FINDINGS OF AN EVALUATION will always be suspect unless the evidence of a program's success (or failure) has been rigorously obtained. Among the causes for concern is how convincingly the evaluator has linked any conclusions about program participation to the program itself, or whether, in fact, another skilled practitioner might have attributed the results to some other activities. Suppose, for example, the claim is made that Program A, a six-month course to teach adults to speak French, is extremely meritorious because of the conversational skills demonstrated by 25 of the 30 participants. If it can also be shown that a special television show offering programming in basic French conversation was available for three of the six months and that the 30 participants actually watched with regularity, the accuracy of the conclusions drawn about Program A may be questioned; it would be hard to determine whether the participants acquired their skills from Program A, the television show, or some combination of both. To ensure that the claims made for a program are valid, the evaluator must have control over the environment under study. The nature of that control or "manipulation" is the subject of the first section of this chapter: evaluation designs. Three basic designs (case, time series, and comparison group) are discussed, and threats to internal and external validity are described.

Once the evaluation's design has been selected, it then becomes necessary to decide who will participate in the study. In some instances, the decision is easy: Everyone gets evaluated. In others, however, it's not so simple. Suppose the evaluation calls for a comparison group design with a time-series component. How many people should be involved in each group to make the evaluation's results convincing and statistically powerful? How many observations over time can you afford with all those people? What happens if you reduce the number of people and observations? The second section of this chapter addresses the issue of sampling and how to select people, places, and events for evaluations.

HOW TO CHOOSE AN EVALUATION DESIGN

A design strategy describes how you will group people and how you will manipulate variables to answer evaluation questions. Sometimes a single design can be used to answer all the questions in an evaluation; sometimes you will need several designs. A classic example of a design strategy is when you separate people into two groups, giving an experimental program to one group and a placebo program to the other.

Evaluators use internal and external validity as the criteria for deciding how accurately a design strategy will answer the evaluation questions. When a design has internal validity, you can distinguish between changes caused by the program you're evaluating and changes resulting from other causes. If an evaluation is comparing two programs to improve the management of mental health centers, for example, and if the administrators in those two programs are not alike at the start, then it will be hard to tell whether any improvements were due to the programs or to differences that already existed between administrators. The design may lack internal validity.

Threats to internal validity include:

- *History:* changes in the environment that occur at the same time as the program

- *Maturation:* changes within individuals that result from natural, biological, or psychological development

- *Testing:* the effects of a premeasure on subsequent measures

- *Instrumentation:* changes in the calibration, administration, or scoring of an instrument from one group or time to the next

- *Statistical regression:* When people are chosen for a program on the basis of their extremely high or low scores on the same selection measure, the high scorers will perform as well and low scorers will perform better if they take the same or similar test a second time.

- *Selection:* the consequences of comparing nonequivalent groups
- *Mortality/Attrition:* the result of participants dropping out of the evaluation

External validity is the criterion for deciding whether an evaluation's findings will hold true for other people in other places. If participants perform better simply because they are excited about taking part in an innovative program (the Hawthorne Effect), then the evaluation design may lack external validity.

All designs must be internally valid. External validity is important whenever your findings are going to be applied to people or settings that were not included in your evaluation, or when findings based on current participants will be used to make decisions affecting future participants.

Threats to external validity include:

- *Reactive effects of testing:* the result of a premeasure(s) making participants sensitive to the aims of a program
- *Interactive effects of selection bias:* how generalizable the evaluation's findings are to other subjects and settings
- *Reactive effects of innovation (Hawthorne Effect):* changes in subjects' performance that result from their excitement about participating in an experimental program or evaluation
- *Multiple-program interference:* difficulty caused in isolating the effects of an experimental program because subjects are concurrently participating in other possibly complementary activities or programs

Figure 1 presents a checklist to help you select the right design strategy for your particular evaluation. To use it, you must study each evaluation question to determine:

- How many groups are being compared?
- Can the groups be considered equivalent at the beginning of the evaluation?
- How many times is each measure administered?

What Is a Case Design?

A case design is used to examine a single, cohesive group. Evaluators typically use case designs to answer questions that ask for a description

How Many Groups Are Being Compared?	How Many Times Is Each Measure Administered?	Are the Groups Being Compared Equivalent at the Beginning of the Evaluation?	Design Strategy to Use
Just one group is involved	Just one time	Does not apply	Case
	Two or more times	Does not apply	Time series
Two or more groups	Just one time	Not equivalent groups	Quasi-experimental comparison group
		Equivalent groups	True experimental comparison group
	Two or more times	Not equivalent groups	Quasi-experimental comparison group and time series
		Equivalent groups	True experimental group and time series

Figure 1   Evaluation Design Selection Checklist

of a program's participants, goals, activities, and results. Questions about new programs or demonstration projects for which comparisons are not yet available almost always require case design strategies.

Most evaluations ask some questions that call for case designs and some that do not. Case designs are sometimes called *preexperimental,* since they are often used to establish the existence of certain factors that, if confirmed, can then be studied in more controlled situations.

Example 41   A Case Design

The state department of social welfare began an equal employment program on a trial basis to help minorities and women get better jobs. At the end of the year, an evaluator was called in to answer questions about the job ranking of minority and female employees. To do this, the evaluator used a case design, interviewing all employees and reviewing employment records. The sequence of activities is depicted in the following diagram:

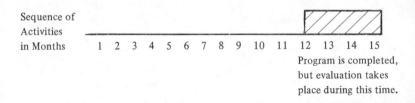

Sequence of
Activities
in Months   1 2 3 4 5 6 7 8 9 10 11 12 13 14 15

Program is completed,
but evaluation takes
place during this time.

Does this design have internal validity? Consider these possibilities:

(1) Some event may occur at the same time as the program that changes employment opportunities.
(2) Employees may change job ranks naturally over the course of a year.
(3) The people who remain employed and in the program may be inherently different from others who are fired or move away. (They might be more skilled, for example.)

Does this design have external validity? In the excitement of the program, employers and employees may temporarily abandon their prejudices toward women and minorities (the Hawthorne Effect). Always be alert to possible threats to the internal and external validity of your evaluation design.

What Is a Time-Series Design?

Time-series evaluation designs involve collecting information about the same group or groups over several periods of time.[1] Time-series designs are especially appropriate when an evaluation question asks you to compare a group's current performance against its past performance. One example of the time-series design is a longitudinal evaluation of the cohesion of families who participated in an experimental family services program. By comparing their cohesion from year to year, you can see what changes have taken place. You can also use time-series designs to find out whether a program has lasting effects. You might do this, for example, by testing students each year for five years after they complete their training to see how well they remember what they learned.

Time-series designs usually cannot guard against the possibility that the effects of some unusual event occurring concurrently with the experimental treatment will be confused with the evaluation findings. But this design (particularly the repeated measures form) is probably most difficult to implement because it's hard to keep track of people over long periods of time and because problems arise when you administer the same measures repeatedly. If the same group is being tracked over time, some participants are likely to drop out at each measurement, seriously reducing the total sample. You also run the risk of having people become too familiar with the contents of the test. When you track different groups, there is another danger: The population you are measuring may change in character from time to time. Most time-series designs are considered *quasi-experimental* because they provide only partial control over threats to internal validity.

Example 42   A Time-Series Evaluation Design

The University Teaching Hospital is conducting an evaluation of a reconstructive surgery program for breast cancer patients using a time-series design. Twice a year for three years, the hospital measures the self-concept, sexual adjustment, and health status of women who had plastic surgery. The evaluation design is depicted in the following diagram.

Time 1 (September, Year 1)	Time 2 (June, Year 1)	Time 3 (September, Year 2)	Time 4 (June, Year 2)	Time 5 (September, Year 3)	Time 6 (June, Year 3)

Does this design have internal validity? Consider these possibilities:

(1) An external event such as the women's movement might change attitudes and affect self-concept and sexual adjustment.
(2) You might find changes in the way the measures were administered from one time to another.

Does this design have external validity? Consider this:

(1) Women may benefit more from their excitement about participating in an experimental program (the Hawthorne effect) than from the surgery itself.
(2) Women participating in the evaluation may not be representative of other breast cancer patients.

What Is a Comparison Group Design?

A strategy often recommended to answer evaluation questions is the comparison group design. This design strategy divides people into two or more groups, with one group participating in the program being evaluated. The others may take part in another program or may not participate in any program (if so, the first group is called the experimental group and the second is called the control group).

Some evaluation questions require a combination of time-series and comparison group designs. If the various groups included in a comparison group design are each measured several times (say every two months for two years), the result is both a time-series design and a comparison group design.

Comparison group designs are frequently divided into two categories: *quasi-* and *true* experimental designs (Campbell and Stanley, 1963). Both categories include comparison groups, but membership in the groups is determined in different ways. In quasi-experimental designs, individuals are assigned to experimental and control groups in such a way that differences may exist between the groups before the program begins. That means any observed differences between them after participation in the program can't be conclusively linked to the experimental program. In true experimental designs, on the other hand, assignment of individuals results in groups that are initially as similar as possible, and any observed differences can be linked to participation in the experimental program. To guarantee the similarity of the groups for a true experimental design, you usually have to assign individuals at random to the various groups.

Example 43   A Quasi-Experimental Comparison Group Design

You have been asked to evaluate two meals-on-wheels programs. Eligible participants can choose to enroll in either program. One of the questions asked by the evaluation is whether participants are satisfied with the size of portions. To answer this question, you asked participants in both groups to complete a questionnaire at the end of the three months' treatment. The evaluation design strategy for this question can be depicted as:

Program 1	Program 2

Is the quasi-experimental comparison group design used in the example above internally valid? Consider these possibilities:

(1) Participants in the two groups may be different from one another at the beginning of the program. For example, more severely disabled persons may choose one program over the other.

(2) Participants who truly disliked the meals may have dropped out of the programs.

The external validity of the design in Example 43 could be threatened by the Hawthorne Effect, or it could be threatened because the participants are not representative.

Example 44   A Quasi-Experimental Comparison Group Design and a Time-Series Design

Another question posed for the evaluation of the two meals-on-wheels programs (Example 43) is whether nutritional balance has improved. To answer this question, you interviewed participants in both programs three times: at the beginning of the year, at the end of the first month, and at the end of the year. This evaluation design strategy can be depicted as:

	Program 1	Program 2
Time 1		
Time 2		
Time 3		

The internal validity of the design in Example 44 may be threatened if persons with serious health problems more often select one program over the other. The design's external validity can be threatened if the measures themselves influence the behavior of people in one of the programs by causing them to be more aware of the nutritional content of their diet. Other threats include the Hawthorne Effect and the possibility that participants in the program are not representative of all people who might possibly benefit from a meals-on-wheels program.

Example 45   A True Experimental Comparison Group Design

The government commissioned an evaluation to determine which of three programs for blind children cost the least. The evaluation used a comparison group design in which children at the Blair Institute were randomly assigned to one of the three programs and the costs of the three programs were compared. The evaluation design is depicted in the following diagram:

	Program 1	Program 2	Program 3
All costs are measured at the conclusion of the program			

The design used in Example 45 probably has no realistic threats to its internal validity. Because children were randomly assigned to each program, any sources of change that might compete with the program's impact would affect all three groups equally.

Its external validity may be threatened, however, because the evaluation findings do not necessarily apply to blind children other than those at Blair Institute. Another possibility is that program administrators and staff may not spend as much money as usual because they know the evaluation involves comparing the cost of their program to its competitors (the Hawthorne Effect).

Example 46   A True Experimental Comparison
Group Design and a Time-Series Design

Programs 1 and 2 in Example 45 proved to be equally cost effective. The government then commissioned an evaluation to determine which program provided the best learning experience. To answer this evaluation question, a comparison group design was selected in which achievement test scores from the beginning and end of the program for children in Programs 1 and 2 were compared. The evaluation design is depicted in the following diagram:

	Time 1 (beginning of program)	Time 2 (end of program)
Program 1		
Program 2		

The design used in Example 46 is probably internally valid. For external validity, you should consider the possibility that the children may react to the tests more than to the programs; that other blind children may not react to the program in the same way as the children at Blair Institute; and that some children may perform better because they are excited about being involved in an innovative program.

SAMPLING

Whenever you sample you are taking a calculated risk. If you do everything correctly, then the risk is negligible and you probably have saved time and money and have avoided a lot of inconvenience for a lot of people.

When you sample you should not be gambling against the odds. The object of sampling is not to beat the odds, but to fix the odds as high as possible in your favor, and to know just what those odds are. So the first rule is simple—Don't gamble:

Do Not Sample . . .

- when it's easier and cheaper to test everyone;
- when you don't have anyone trained in proper sampling methods;
- when you don't have the time or money to use the proper sampling methods;
- when you need information more precise than the mathematical approximations the sample will yield; or
- when it will cost you more time and effort than the information is worth to the people paying for the evaluation.

A sample should be a miniature version of the population to which the evaluation findings are going to be applied. Unfortunately, human beings are a notoriously shifty and complex population; they are difficult to pin down and classify. As a result many different methods of sampling have been developed to suit different occasions. These include:

- Simple Random Sampling
- Stratified Random Sampling
- Simple Random Cluster Sampling
- Paired-Selections Cluster Sampling
- Simple Random Item Sampling
- Simple Random Item-Examinee Sampling
- Multiple Matrix Sampling

Simple Random Sampling

Say you have six student nurses, and their test scores are as follows:

Student	Score
1	9
2	8
3	4
4	10
5	9
6	2

Variance = 8.64
Standard Deviation (SD) = 2.94

If you choose as a sample just two of the students, then there are 15 possible score combinations you can come up with. In this case, the combinations and their mean scores would look like this:

Sample	Mean Score	Sample	Mean Score
1,2	8.5	2,6	5.0
1,3	6.5	3,4	7.0
1,4	9.5	3,5	6.5
1,5	9.0	3,6	3.0
1,6	5.5	4,5	9.5
2,3	6.0	4,6	6.0
2,4	9.0	5,6	5.5
2,5	8.5		

$\overline{X} = 105/15 = 7.0$
Standard Error (SE) = 1.8

The mean score for the total population of students is 7.0. Note that only one of the samples of two students produces such a mean. A sample will give you a mean score only approximating the true mean; how exact that approximation is depends on your sample size and how much the population varies. (But remember, a bigger sample doesn't always mean a better sample.)

You can measure the accuracy of a particular sampling method by computing the standard error (SE) of the mean. For the preceding example, the mean scores for the 15 samples range from 3.0 to 9.5. The standard deviation of these means—all of which are approximations of the population mean—is the standard error of estimate. In this case, the average of the 15 means is 7.0, exactly the same as the population average. The SE is 1.8. This tells you that an estimated mean will be on the average ± 1.79 points from the true population mean. As the sample size increases, the SE decreases.

The formula for computing the standard error is as follows:

$$SE = \sqrt{[(N - n)/(N - 1)] \text{ Variance}/n}$$

where

    N = total population size

    n = sample size

and

$$\text{Variance} = \sum_{i=1}^{N} \frac{(X_i - \bar{X})^2}{N} = \text{Variance in the total population}$$

Effects of sample size on the SE:

n =	then	SE =
1		2.9
2		1.8
3		1.3
4		.9
5		.6
6		0.0

Example 47   An Elderly Care Seminar.

Two hundred nurses, therapists, and social workers employed by a midwest city signed up for an experimental elderly care seminar. The city, however, only had enough money to pay for 50 participants. The seminar director therefore assigned each candidate a number from 001 to 200 and, using a table of random numbers, selected 50 names by moving down columns of 3-digit random numbers and taking the first 50 numbers within the range 001 to 200. (The director also decided this method was easier than picking numbers from a hat.)

The advantages of simple random sampling are:

- simplest of all sampling methods and easiest to conduct
- most computers have built-in tables for drawing a random sample

The disadvantages of simple random sampling are:

- produces greater standard errors than do other sampling methods
- cannot be used if you want to break subjects down into subgroups (for example, 60% male and 40% female)

Stratified Random Sampling

In simple random sampling you choose a subset (n) of subjects at random from a population of N. In stratified random sampling, you first subdivide population N into subgroups or strata and then select a given number of subjects from each stratum to get a sample n.

You can use stratified random sampling to get, say, an equal representation of males and females. You do this by dividing the entire group into subgroups of males and females and then randomly choosing a given number of subjects from each subgroup. This method of sampling can be more precise than simple random sampling—but only if you choose the strata properly.

Stratified random sampling attempts to increase accuracy by homogenizing the groups to be sampled. Suppose that the same six students used in the previous table were grouped so that students 1, 4, and 5 were assigned to one strata and students 2, 3, and 6 to another. The strata could represent different programs, different age groups, or different achievement groups.

The estimated means that result if you were to randomly choose one student from each strata (two students in all) are listed on p. 93. As you can see, the means are closer to the population mean of 7.0 than they were with simple random sampling.

In both cases, the average of the estimated means is exactly the same as the average of the population, 7.0. However, with stratified random

| (Student Number) | | |
Stratum 1	Stratum 2	Mean
1	2	8.6
1	3	6.5
1	6	5.5
4	2	9.0
4	3	7.0
4	6	6.0
5	2	8.5
5	3	6.5
5	6	5.5

$\overline{X} = 7.0$
SE = 1.3

sampling, the standard error is lower. In general, a decrease in the SE will result only if the strata are carefully chosen to reflect a real, and not an arbitrary, distinction—that is, the strata must be *meaningful*. (Note that in the preceding example the strata divided higher- and lower-scoring students.)

One way to test for meaningful strata is by assigning a value of 1 to the first strata, 2 to the second strata, and so on, and then correlating sample test scores with strata values. If you get high positive or negative correlations, you probably have useful strata.

The formula for computing the standard error of estimate for stratified random sampling is as follows:

$$SE = \sqrt{\left(\frac{1}{N^2}\right) \sum_{i=1}^{I} \frac{[N_i^2 (N_i - n_i) \text{ Variance}_i]}{(N_i - 1)n_i}}$$

where

I = number of strata

N = population size

N_i = total number of subjects in stratum i before sampling

n_i = number of subjects sampled from stratum i

Variance_i = variance of all subjects in stratum i before sampling

Example 48   A Smoking Cessation Program

The University Health Center developed a new program to help young people quit smoking. The administration commissioned an evaluation to find out, among other things, how effective the program was with male and female undergraduates of different ages.

The evaluation used a comparison group design comparing the new program to the Health Center's old quit-smoking program, taking into account participants' sex and age. Some 310 undergraduates signed up for the Health Center's old quit-smoking program for the winter seminar. Of the 310, 140 were between 17 and 20 years old, and 62 of these were men. Some 170 students were between 21 and 23, and 80 of these were men. The evaluators randomly selected 40 persons from each of the four subgroups and randomly assigned every other student to the new program and the remainder to the old program. The design looked like this:

| | Age 17-22 | | Age 21-24 | |
	Male	Female	Male	Female
New program	20	20	20	20
Old program	20	20	20	20

The advantages of stratified random sampling are:

- can be more precise than simple random sampling
- permits evaluator to choose a sample that represents various groups in desired proportions

The disadvantages of stratified random sampling are:

- requires more effort than simple random sampling
- often needs a larger sample size than a simple random sample would to produce statistically meaningful results
- the modest standard error decrease caused by stratification can usually be obtained by slightly increasing sample size in a simple random sample

Simple Random Cluster Sampling

Simple random cluster sampling is used primarily for administrative convenience, not to improve sampling precision. Sometimes random selection cannot be used—for example, when it would interrupt every hospital ward to choose just a few patients from each ward for a testing program. Also, sometimes random selection of individuals can be unethical or administratively impossible.

One solution to the problem of using, say, individuals as the sampling unit is to use groups or clusters of subjects instead of individuals. This is the purpose of simple random cluster sampling—to avoid being randomly obtrusive.

In simple random sampling, you randomly select a subset of subjects from all possible individuals who might take part in an evaluation. Cluster sampling is analogous to random sampling, except that groups rather than individuals are assigned randomly. This method presupposes that the population is organized into natural or predefined clusters or groups.

Suppose that 30 project directors studying finance are divided into six practice groups, each group containing five persons. The following table shows directors and cluster scores on a 10-item competency test in finance:

Project Director	Cluster						
	1	2	3	4	5	6	
1	8	7	8	6	7	6	
2	9	9	6	2	1	1	
3	7	7	9	3	8	4	$\bar{X} = 6.0$
4	9	5	8	5	2	7	
5	6	6	7	8	4	5	

The evaluator wants to get an estimate of the mean score in the total population of 30 project directors by testing just some of them. In this case the evaluator decides to select randomly two out of the six practice groups, since testing two intact groups is preferable to disrupting practice in all six groups.

The following table shows the mean scores on the competency test in finance from each of the possible sets of two clusters:

Sample (Combination of Clusters)	Mean Score
1,2	7.3
1,3	7.7
1,4	6.3
1,5	6.1
1,6	6.2
2,3	7.2
2,4	5.8
2,5	5.6
2,6	5.7
3,4	6.2
3,5	6.0
3,6	6.1
4,5	4.6
4,6	4.7
5,6	4.5

$\overline{X} = 6.0$
SE = .91

Note that the average of the estimates from all possible sampling combinations is 6.0 (the actual mean in the total population), and the standard deviation of the estimated means, or the standard error of estimate is .91. The standard error also could have been computed using the following formula:

$$SE = \sqrt{\left(\frac{N-n}{Nn}\right)\left(\frac{NM-1}{M^2N-M^2}\right)[1+(M-1)Rho]\ Var(X)}$$

where

N = total number of clusters

M = number of persons in each cluster

n = number of clusters sampled randomly

Var(X) = variance of test scores in the total population

Rho = intraclass correlation coefficient (the correlation among clusters)

The following example uses clusters with the same number of subjects to simplify the calculations.[2]

Example 49 Family Counseling Groups in a Mental Health Center

The Community Mental Health Center had 40 separate family counseling groups, each with about 30 participants. The directors noticed a decline in attendance in the past year and decided to try out an experimental program where each individual would be tested and interviewed separately before therapy began. The program was very expensive, and the center's directors could afford to finance only a 150-person program at first.

Randomly selecting individuals from all group members would have created friction and disturbed the integrity of some of the groups. Instead the evaluator suggested a simple random cluster sampling plan in which five of the groups—150 people altogether—would be randomly selected to take part in the experimental program. Each group would be treated as a cluster. At the end of six months, the progress of the experimental subjects would be compared with that of the subjects treated in the traditional way.

The advantages of simple random cluster sampling are:

- can be used when it is inconvenient or unethical to randomly select individual subjects
- administratively simple since no identification of individuals is necessary

The disadvantages of simple random cluster sampling are:

- not mathematically efficient. Note that for any given number of subjects tested, the more clusters, the smaller the standard error. One subject in each cluster would be the equivalent of simple random sampling

Paired-Selections Cluster Sampling

Simple random cluster sampling is a modified version of simple random sampling. The difference is whether the sampling unit is a group or an individual. In simple random sampling you randomly select a subset of n people from a population of N. In simple cluster sampling, the total population of n is organized into L groups or clusters, and you randomly select some of the clusters to get a sample size of n.

Similarly, paired-selections cluster sampling is a modified version of stratified random sampling. For stratified random sampling, you first divide a population of N into strata and randomly select a given number of subjects from each stratum. In paired-selections cluster sampling, the total population of N already is divided into L clusters, and you further subdivide it into strata and then randomly select two clusters from each stratum, ending up with a sample size n. Thus in paired-selections cluster sampling, a group is the sampling unit and only two clusters are selected from each stratum.

Suppose for example that each of the practice groups in the finance program for project directors evaluation was stratified so that clusters 1, 2, and 3 were assigned to one stratum and clusters 4, 5, and 6 were assigned to the other stratum. The strata could segregate, say, different experience or educational levels. The following table shows the estimated means that would result if you were to randomly select two practice groups from each stratum, or four clusters in all:

Strata		Mean
1	2	
1,2	4,5	5.95
1,2	4,6	6.00
1,2	5,6	5.90
2,3	4,5	5.90
2,3	4,6	5.95
2,3	5,6	5.85
1,3	4,5	6.15
1,3	4,6	6.20
1,3	5,6	6.10

$\overline{X} = 6.00$
SE = .12

Comparing this table with the table for simple random cluster sampling, you can see that in this case the means are closer to the population mean of 6.0 (ranging from 5.90 to 6.20).

In both cases the average of the estimated means is exactly the same as the average in the total population, 6.0. However, with paired-selections cluster sampling, the standard error of estimate is lower. This usually will hold true if the strata are meaningful—that is, if the clusters within each stratum more closely resemble each other than they do the clusters in other strata.

Once again, a formula is available for determining the standard error of estimate:

$$SE = \sqrt{\left(\frac{b-2}{2N}\right)\left(\frac{CV_{ws}}{M^2}\right)}$$

where

N = total number of clusters

M = number of persons in each cluster

b = number of clusters within each stratum

CV_{ws} = component of variance within strata (from an analysis of variance)

Example 50   An Experimental Dental Hygiene Program

Barton School District had just received a grant to try out an experimental dental hygiene program, but there was not enough money to set up the program in all of the district's 25 elementary schools. The district board therefore decided to choose ten schools in which to try out the program, with the remaining schools acting as controls.

The evaluators noted that research showed a high correlation between good dental hygiene and family income, and demographic records showed large differences among the income levels of students' families from school to school. The evaluators therefore decided to use a paired-selections cluster sampling strategy.

First, they ranked each school's sixth grade class (the clusters) according to family income. Next, they formed strata by taking in rank order $2(N)/a$ clusters, where a = total number of clusters to be sampled, and N = total number of clusters. In this case a = 10 and N = 25, and consequently $(2)(25)/(10)$, or 5 strata were created. The first stratum consisted of the five sixth grade classes with the highest average family incomes; the second, the next five highest average income classes; and so on. Finally, the evaluator randomly selected two classes from each stratum.

The advantages and disadvantages of simple random cluster sampling also hold true for paired-selections cluster sampling.

Simple Random Item Sampling

So far we have discussed sampling plans that involved selecting individuals or groups of individuals to take part in evaluations. Simple random item sampling is concerned instead with the items that are used to test individuals.

Say you have 250 possible questions to ask for your evaluation, but only time enough to ask 50. Using simple random item sampling, you randomly select k (in this case 50) items for your test from a total population of K (in this case 250) items. (The collection of total available items is called an item pool.)

The following table shows the scores each of six students obtained on a total item pool of six items designed to measure dental hygiene knowledge:

Student	Item 1	2	3	4	5	6	Test Score	
1	0	1	1	1	1	1	5	
2	1	1	0	1	0	0	3	
3	1	1	1	0	1	0	4	
4	0	0	0	0	1	0	1	$\overline{X} = 3.2$
5	0	1	1	1	0	1	4	
6	0	1	0	0	1	0	2	
	2	5	3	3	4	2		

Example 51 shows the estimated mean scores and standard errors of estimate resulting from different sample sizes (k = 1 to k = 6).

Example 51 Estimated Mean Scores for Different Simple Random Item Sampling Plans

k = 1 Items	k = 1 Estimated Mean	k = 2 Items	k = 2 Estimated Mean	k = 3 Items	k = 3 Estimated Mean	k = 4 Items	k = 4 Estimated Mean	k = 5 Items	k = 5 Estimated Mean	k = 6 Items	k = 6 Estimated Mean
1	2	1,2	3.5	1,2,3	3.3	1,2,3,4	3.2	2,3,4,5,6	3.4	1,2,3,4,5,6	3.2
2	5	1,3	2.5	1,2,4	3.3	1,2,3,5	3.5	1,3,4,5,6	2.8		
3	3	1,4	2.5	1,2,5	3.7	1,2,3,6	3.0	1,2,4,5,6	3.2		
4	3	1,5	3.0	1,2,6	3.0	1,2,4,5	3.5	1,2,3,5,6	3.2		
5	4	1,6	2.0	2,3,4	3.7	1,2,4,6	3.0	1,2,3,4,6	3.0		
6	2	2,3	4.0	2,3,5	4.0	1,2,5,6	3.2	1,2,3,4,5	3.4		
		2,4	4.0	2,3,6	3.3	1,3,4,5	3.0				
		2,5	4.5	3,4,5	3.3	1,3,4,6	2.5				
		2,6	3.5	3,4,6	2.7	1,3,5,6	2.8				
		3,4	3.0	1,3,4	2.7	1,4,5,6	2.8				
		3,5	3.5	1,3,5	3.0	2,3,4,5	3.8				
		3,6	2.5	1,3,6	2.3	2,3,4,6	3.2				
		4,5	3.5	1,4,5	3.0	2,3,5,6	3.5				
		4,6	2.5	1,4,6	2.3	2,4,5,6	3.5				
		5,6	3.0	1,5,6	2.7	3,4,5,6	3.0				
				2,4,5	4.0						
				2,4,6	3.3						
				2,5,6	3.7						
				3,5,6	3.0						
				4,5,6	3.0						
$\bar{X}$ = 3.20			3.20		3.20		3.20		3.20		3.20
SE = 1.07			.68		.48		.33		.21		.00

101

The formula for estimating the mean test score in the total examinee population for item sampling is as follows:

$$\bar{X} = K \left(\frac{N}{2}\right) \left(\frac{k}{2}\right) \frac{X_{ij}}{Nk}$$

$$i=1 \quad j=1$$

where

K = total number of items in the item pool

N = total number of examinees

k = number of items sampled

X_{ij} = score of examinee i on item j

As in simple random sampling with individuals, the average of the estimated means is the same for each value of k and equal to the mean in the total population, 3.2 (see Example 51). Also, as the sample size increases (k gets larger), the standard error of estimate decreases. The equation for the standard error is as follows:

$$SE = \sqrt{K^2 \left(\frac{K - k}{K}\right) \frac{CV_I}{k}}$$

where

k = number of items sampled

K = total number of items in item pool

CV_I = component of variance for items (derived from an analysis of variance)

The standard errors of estimate usually are smaller for simple random item sampling than for simple random sampling of examinees. That is, given an item pool K, and an examinee population size K, you get smaller standard erors if you try out k items on all individuals than if you randomly select k persons to answer all items. This happens because generally there is less variation among people on any given item than among people across all items. It also explains why a given sampling plan can produce different standard errors of estimate when used with different individuals or sets of items.

The advantages of simple random item sampling are:

- can save test-taking time
- reduces testing burden on examinees

The disadvantages of simple random item sampling are:

- requires a large and thoroughly validated item pool

Simple Random Item-Examinee Sampling

In simple random item-examinee sampling, you draw a random sample of k of K items to administer to a random sample of N examinees. You use the data collected to estimate the average test score you would get if you administered all possible items (K) to all possible examinees (N). The following table shows the scores of six examinees on six items.

			Item				Test
Student	1	2	3	4	5	6	Score
1	1	1	1	1	0	1	5
2	1	1	1	1	1	1	6
3	1	1	1	1	1	1	6
4	0	1	1	0	0	0	2
5	1	0	1	1	0	0	3
6	0	1	1	0	0	0	2
	4	5	6	4	2	3	

$\bar{X} = 4.00$

For the sake of simplicity, suppose this represents all examinees and all items, and you want to take a sample of three examinees and three items (k = 3, K = 6; n = 3, N = 6). The formula for estimating the mean test score in the total population would be:

$$\bar{X} = K \sum_{i=1}^{n} \sum_{j=1}^{k} \frac{X_{ij}}{nk}$$

where

K = total number of items in the item pool

n = number of examinees sampled

k = number of items sampled

X_{ij} = score of examinee i on item j

You could choose 400 different combinations of three items and three examinees. If you had randomly selected, say, examinees 1, 3, and 5 and items 2, 4, and 6, the estimated mean examinee/item combination would be 6 [3 + 3 + 1]/[(3)(3)] = 4.67. Note that this value, 4.67, is much higher than the actual mean value, 4.00. However, the average of all 400 means would equal 4.00.

To find the standard error of estimate (SE), you could compute the standard deviation for all 400 possible mean scores, or you could use the following formula, which in this case tells you that SE = 1.07:

$$SE = \sqrt{K^2 \left[\frac{(N-n)CV_E}{Nn} + \frac{(K-k)CV_I}{Kk} + \frac{(N-n)(K-k)CV_{IE}}{NKnk} \right]}$$

where

K = total number of items in the item pool

N = total number of possible examinees

k = number of items sampled

n = number of examinees sampled

CV_E, CV_I, CV_{IE} = components of variance for examinees, items, and item-by-examinee interaction derived from analysis of variance

Example 52   Nurses' Perceptions of an In-Service Training Program

The Memorial Medical Center wanted to know what its nurses thought of the center's in-service training program. The program evaluator had an item pool of 100 attitudinal questions, each individually validated. In order to limit the burden on the nurses, the evaluator used a simple random item-examinee sampling strategy, randomly selecting 12 of the 100 items to administer to a random sample of 20 nurses.

The advantages of simple random item-examinee sampling are:

● permits sampling of both individuals and items at once

The disadvantages of simple random item-examinee sampling are:

● can be administratively and mathematically cumbersome

Multiple Matrix Sampling

In item-examinee sampling, you use only subset n of persons and subset k of items. In multiple matrix sampling, however, you randomly select more than one combination of items and examinees, then merge the test results from each combination to get a single estimate of the mean score in the total population and item pool.

For example, for the table on page 103, where the total item pool (K) = 6 and the total examinee population (N) = 6, you could divide the item pool into two unique, randomly constructed subtests, each containing three items. Say you chose items 2, 3, and 5 for subtest 1 and items 1, 4, and 6 for subtest 2. You then would divide the examinee population at random into unique subgroups—into subgroup 1 containing, say, examinees 1, 2, and 4, and subgroup 2, containing examinees 3, 5, and 6. You then would give subtest 1 to all examinees in subgroup 1, and subtest 2 to all examinees in subgroup 2.

You don't have to divide the total item pool into just two subtests—you could have three, four, five, or six subtests with different numbers of examinees in each subgroup. Also, you need not include all examinees; you can select a sample of examinees and then divide them into subgroups.

You get the total estimated mean score by calculating the mean in each subgroup and then combining these means to produce an estimated mean for the total population. You can use the following formula to compute the estimated mean score.

$$\bar{X} = \frac{\sum\limits_{i=1}^{t} \text{Mean}_i \, n_i \, k_i}{\sum\limits_{i=1}^{t} n_i \, k_i}$$

where

t = number of subtests

n_i = number of examinees responding to subtest i

K_i = number of items in subtest i

Mean_i = mean for particular item/examinees grouping administered subtest i

In the previous example, $t = 2$ (there are two subtests: items 2, 3, and 5 and items 1, 4, and 6; $k_1 = k_2 = 3$ (each subtest has three items); and $n_1 = n_2 =$ (three examinees in each subgroup: persons 1, 2, and 4 and persons 3, 5, and 6). You can calculate the mean for the subgroups by using the previous formula for item-examinee sampling, in this case:

Mean 1 = subgroup 1/subtest 1 = $(6)(2 + 3 + 2)/(3)(3) = 4.67$
Mean 2 = subgroup 2/subtest 2 = $(6)(3 + 2 + 0)/(3)(3) = 3.33$

You can then calculate the estimated mean for the total population as follows:

$$\frac{(4.67)/(3)(3) + (3.33)(3)(3)}{(3)(3) + (3)(3)} = 4.00$$

This estimated mean is just one of 200 you could calculate based on dividing the item pool into two equal-sized subtests and assigning three examinees at random to each subtest. For example, another combination—subtest 1 = items 1, 2, and 5 and subtest 2 = items 3, 4, and 6, with subgroup 1 = examinees 1, 3, and 5 and subgroup 2 = examinees 2, 4, and 6—yields an estimated mean of 3.67.

In general, you can calculate the standard error of estimate with the following formula:

$$SE = \sqrt{K^2 \left[\frac{(N-tn)CV_E}{Ntn} + \frac{(K-tk)CV_I}{Ktk} + \frac{(NK-nK-Nk+tkn)CV_{IE}}{NKtnk} \right]}$$

where

K = number of items in the item pool

N = number of examinees in the total population

n = number of examinees sampled

k = number of items sampled

t = number of subtests

CV_E, CV_I, CV_{IE} = components of variance for examinees, items, and item-by-examinee interaction derived from analysis of variance

Example 53   The Heart Association's Community Education Program

The Heart Association hired an evaluator to assess its community education program. One evaluation question asked how the program affected the knowledge of nutrition of 200 high school students attending a recent seminar.

The evaluator found a standardized, validated 80-item test. To limit the testing time to 15 minutes a student, the evaluator designed a multiple matrix sampling plan, randomly dividing the 80-item test into four 20-item subtests and the 200 students into four subgroups of 50 each. The evaluator then randomly matched each subgroup with a subtest and gave the assigned subtest to every student in each group.

The advantages of multiple matrix sampling are:

- reduction in testing burden because each examinee answers only a subset of items from the item pool; but also permits more compre-

Technique	Who Gets Sampled	Advantages	Disadvantages
Simple Random Sampling: A subset of n individuals is chosen at random from a population of N individuals.	Individuals	• Simplest of all sampling methods • Many computers have built-in programs for drawing random samples	• Produces greater standard errors than other sampling methods • Cannot be used when you need to sample by subgroups (e.g., 60% men, 40% women)
Stratified Random Sampling: The population (N) is subdivided into subgroups or strata, and then, a given number of individuals are selected at random from each stratum to get a sample of size n.	Individuals	• Can be more precise than random sampling • Permits evaluator to choose a sample that represents various groups in desired populations	• Requires more effort than simple random sampling • Often needs a larger sample size than a simple random sample to produce statistically meaningful results
Simple Random Cluster Sampling: A subset of n groups is chosen at random from a population of N groups.	Groups	• Can be used when it is inconvenient or unethical to randomly select individual subjects • Administratively simple since no identification of individuals is necessary	• Not mathematically efficient
Paired-Selection Cluster Sampling: The population of K individuals is divided into L clusters. The clusters are arranged into strata and from each strata two clusters are selected at random.	Groups	Same as for simple random cluster sampling, but also allows you to study groups in some desired proportion	Same as for simple random cluster sampling but you need an even larger sample for statistically meaningful results

Method	Sampling	Advantages	Disadvantages
Simple Random Item Sampling: k items are randomly selected from a population of K items to get a sample size of k and administered to all N examinees.	Items	• Can save time • Reduces testing burden on examinees	• Requires a large and validated item pool
Simple Random Item-Examinee Sampling: k items are randomly selected from K items and given to n examinees selected at random for a population of N examinees.	Items and Individuals	• Permits sampling on two fronts	• Administratively and mathematically cumbersome
Multiple Matrix Sampling: More than one combination of randomly selected items and individuals are formed and the results of each combination are merged.	Items and Individuals	• Reduces testing burden on examinees • Allows comprehensive testing • May produce the precise estimates among all sampling	• Extremely complex to administer • Requires the creation of many valid items and subtests • Cannot be used to assess individuals • Norms associated with standardized tests are not useful

Figure 2 A Summary of Sampling Methods

hensive testing since more items can be used than if each student had to respond to every item

- estimates of group achievement are more precise (smaller standard error) than in other plans

The disadvantages of multiple matrix sampling are:

- complicated procedure
- not as effective for assessing individuals as for assessing groups
- norms accompanying standardized tests may not be of value since not all possible tests items are answered.

Figure 2 presents a summary of sampling methods used in evaluations.

NOTES

1. "The essence of the time-series design is the presence of a periodic measurement process on some group or individual" (Campbell and Stanley, 1971). Time-series designs in which the same group is measured more than once are often called *repeated measures*. Different groups can also be measured in a time-series design.

2. A complete description of simple random cluster sampling with unequal cluster sizes can be found in Cochran (1977).

Collecting Information

THE COLLECTION OF INFORMATION for evaluations is composed of numerous very important activities. Among them are the selection, development, and validation of strategies for measurement—instruments—hiring and training data collectors, and organizing the collected information for data analysis. In this chapter, each of these activities is addressed and emphasis is given to some of the most frequently used data collection tasks.

In the first section, the range of information collection techniques available to the evaluator is described. Next, the validation of data collection strategies is discussed. The third section is concerned with issues surrounding field work: how to hire and train data collectors and how to organize the data that are returned to the evaluator. The next four sections tell how to construct and use several of the most important measuring devices: achievement tests, multiple-choice items, questionnaires, and interviews. In the eighth section, we describe how to use simulations, a relatively new measurement strategy. The last section of this chapter is devoted to the evaluation of attitudes.

HOW TO COLLECT
EVALUATION INFORMATION

You can collect evaluation information in many different ways. If you need information to find out whether a new appointment-making system provides improved service in a large medical clinic, for example, you could use any of the following information collection techniques:

- Give patients a rating scale on which to assess their satisfaction with the appointment service.

- Observe clerks as they book appointments.

- Send questionnaires to clerks to get their opinions about any improvements in appointment making.

- Interview nurses and physicians to ask their opinion about appointment-making efficiency.

- Have clerk supervisors keep a record of how many appointments each clerk books in a day.

- Monitor telephone records to determine amount of busy signals and waiting time.

- Audit appointment records for number of filled and unfilled appointments, cancellations, and no-shows.

This list illustrates five alternative techniques the evaluator might use to get information about improved services: interviews, questionnaires, rating scales, observations, and record reviews. To choose the best one, you should consider four factors.

First, the information collection technique should be agreeable to your client and colleagues. If you wanted to use questionnaires to evaluate the appointment system, for example, but the practice's management preferred interviews, you would have to decide just how serious the consequences of imposing your own choice might be. Second, the information collection techniques should be technically sound and the data collected from them should be reliable, valid, and targeted to the evaluation questions. Third, they should provide the best data the evaluation budget can afford, which means that you will have to decide such things as whether to buy or develop your own measures, and whether to use more than one technique for each evaluation question. Fourth, you must be sure that the methods you choose will allow enough time for gathering and analyzing the data. Major strategies used to collect information for evaluation of health programs are: written self-report measures, observations, interviews, performance tests, record reviews, and written tests of ability.

What About Written Self-Report Measures?

Written self-report measures ask people to tell about their attitudes, beliefs, feelings, and perceptions. Questionnaires, rating and ranking scales, the Semantic Differential, the Q-sort, and diaries are among the techniques most frequently used in program evaluation.

Questionnaires are self-administered survey forms that consist of a set of questions. Answers to questionnaire items can require free responses (short answers) or they can be structured into forced choices (multiple-choice items). Questionnaires are frequently used in large-scale evaluations to obtain participants' reactions and opinions. They are less expensive to construct than most measures, but the kind of information you can get from them is limited, and people don't always answer the questions truthfully. Don't forget that you will have to follow up on those who don't respond, and that's an expensive undertaking.

Rating scales can be used for self-assessment or for appraisals of other people, groups events, or products. For example, you could rate the efficiency of the new appointment system on a 5-point scale from 1 for not very efficient to 5 for very efficient. Rating scales are particularly useful when you need to reduce judgmental data to a manageable form. They are relatively easy to complete and they produce relatively objective data. Unfortunately, they are subject to many types of bias— some raters are lenient and others are not, and sometimes raters let their personal feelings influence their ratings (a halo effect). Further, the amount of information you can obtain from rating scales is limited because the rating categories are never perfect.

Ranking scales involve putting a set of items into a hierarchy according to some value or preference. Asking a pharmacist to rank four drugs from one to four according to their potency in treating headaches is an example. Like rating scales, ranking scales are easy to complete and produce objectified data. But remember that rank ordering a long list of items is no fun and it takes a lot of time. Ranking scales sometimes ask people to make distinctions among things where they can't really see any difference.

Semantic Differential is used to measure attitudes by relying on the indirect meaning of words. For example, parents might be asked to rate their child's teachers using a series of 7-point scales like the following:

Caring	___	___	___	___	___	___	___	Unconcerned
Rushed	___	___	___	___	___	___	___	Relaxed
Pleasant	___	___	___	___	___	___	___	Disagreeable
Confident	___	___	___	___	___	___	___	Inexperienced

The Semantic Differential is relatively easy to complete, it produces objectified data, and respondents usually find it harder to choose "socially acceptable" answers than when they use an ordinary rating scale. However, the Differential can be quite difficult to score.

The Q-sort requires individuals to place a series of items or statements into rating categories so that some minimum number of items is assigned to each category. For example, nursing educators could be asked to rate ten textbooks as above average or below average so that at least two texts are assigned to each category (the remaining texts can be rated either way).

Q-sorts produce objectified data and they force respondents to establish priorities among items that are being compared in an evaluation. But the Q-sort requires people to make very difficult distinctions, the directions are often hard to follow, and the resulting data can require complex analysis methods.

Diary techniques ask people to keep daily or weekly accounts of specific behaviors, attitudes, thoughts, or events. The critical incident technique asks people to record only those things that are particularly important, unique, useful, or revelatory. For example, you could ask patients to keep a diary for two months describing difficulties they encountered because of their asthma. Diaries and critical incidents permit people to describe unique situations in their own words, but people sometimes forget to maintain them and they are often difficult to score and interpret.

Why Not Try Observations?

Another information collection technique frequently used in evaluations is an eyewitness account of individual behavior or program activities. You could use observations, for example, to find out how many patients read the medical literature available in a waiting room. The information collected by observers can be reported by checklists, rating scales, field notes, and summary reports.

Standardized observations require careful planning so that the information obtained is accurate. Observations can give information collectors first-hand information about a program, and they are often the only feasible and economical way to gather certain kinds of information. But it is costly to train observers, and several may be needed to get reliable results. Another drawback is that people who know they are being observed may not behave normally.

Time-sampling observations involve repeated observations of a given situation. For example, observers may note which participants in a continuing education program ask questions during ten consecutive

5-minute intervals. Time sampling allows first-hand observations of a program, and the many observations make it possible to identify unusual events that you might otherwise think were routine occurrences. When all the observations are made one after the other, however, they are likely to depict only one particular situation and not the program as a whole.

Are Interviews Feasible?

An interview is an information collection technique in which one person talks to another or to a group. Interviews can be completely unstructured and spontaneous, or you can decide ahead of time the kinds of questions to ask. If you use multiple-choice questions, even the response categories are predetermined.

Face-to-face interviews might be used, for example, to find out why participants dropped out of a program, and might consist of three basic questions with a series of two or more in-depth questions for each basic question asked. The best thing about the face-to-face interview is that it permits you to probe sensitive subjects such as attitudes or values. But these interviews are usually time consuming and expensive, and you will have to give interviewers special training.

Telephone interviews also permit in-depth probing of sensitive issues and are less costly than face-to-face interviews. They are still expensive compared to questionnaires, however. You should also remember that not everyone has a telephone, and some people are reluctant to reveal their feelings or give personal information over the phone.

Are Performance Tests the Answer?

Performance tests require people to complete a task or make something; then you assess the quality of the performance or product. One example of a performance test is videotaping a session between a psychiatrist and a patient and then having experts view the tape and rate the physician's skills using a specially designed scale.

The major advantage of performance testing is that it relies on tasks that are close to real-world activities. It is often very time consuming and expensive, however, because performance tests generally have to be administered individually and they sometimes require the use of special equipment.

Would Record Reviews Be Enough?

Record reviews mean that you collect evaluation information by going through program-related documents. In a weight reduction program, for example, you might review attendance records to see if participants came to group sessions regularly and medical records to find out about weight loss.

Record reviews are "unobtrusive" in the sense that they do not interfere with the activities of the program being evaluated. They can also be relatively inexpensive because no new data collection is required. One problem is that program documents may be disorganized, unavailable, or incomplete.

Should You Use Written Tests of Ability or Knowledge?

Written achievement tests are among the most commonly used measurement techniques. Achievement tests measure competency in a given subject. They can be developed by the program or evaluation staff or you can buy them from publishers. Achievement tests can be used to measure a diverse range of factors from knowledge of anatomy to skill in taking a patient's history.

The advantages of achievement tests are that they can be administered to large groups at relatively low cost and that carefully developed and validated tests are available in many subject areas. One disadvantage is that achievement tests must be properly validated to provide accurate information, and this can be a costly procedure. Another is that having high scores on a test of factual knowledge doesn't always mean that the individual can apply that knowledge.

Figure 3 summarizes the advantages and limitations of major information collection alternatives for evaluators.

HOW TO VALIDATE EVALUATION INSTRUMENTS

Before you begin collecting information for evaluating a program you should be sure that the instruments you will use—whether questionnaires, interviews, knowledge tests, or whatever—have been validated through field testing and possibly by expert review as well.

Information Collection Alternatives		Advantages	Disadvantages
Observations	Standard Observations	Can observe events first hand	Observers can change the environment
			Inter- and intra-observer reliability can be difficult to obtain
	Time Sampling Observations	Can observe events first hand	Observers can change the environment
		More opportunities to observe	Inter- and intra-observer reliability can be difficult to obtain
Interviews	Face-to-face Interviews	Permits in-depth probing	Costly
		Sensitive issues can be discussed	Inter- and intrarater reliability can be difficult to obtain
	Telephone Interviews	Permits in-depth probing	Costly
		Sensitive issues can be discussed	Some people may not have telephones
		Less costly than face-to-face interviews	More difficult to probe or discuss sensitive issues
Performance Tests		Close to real-world situations	Costly
			Generally must be administered individually
			Can require special equipment or apparatus
Record Review		Unobtrusive	Documents may be disorganized or unavailable
		Can be inexpensive	
		No new data collection required	

Figure 3   Information Collection Alternatives   *(continued)*

Information Collection Alternatives		Advantages	Disadvantages
Written Tests of Ability	Achievement Tests	Can be administered to large groups at relatively low costs Many published, standardized tests are available	Expensive to develop and validate High scores do not necessarily imply that the tested knowledge can be applied
Written Self-Report Measures	Questionnaires	Can be administered to large groups at relatively low costs	Can be difficult to obtain sensitive information Respondents may not always be truthful Must follow-up to obtain adequate numbers of respondents
	Rating Scales	Easy to complete Produces objectified data Reduces judgmental data into a manageable form	Responses may be biased because some raters are lenient and other are strict Amount of information obtainable is circumscribed by the rating categories Halo effect
	Ranking Scales	Easy to complete Produces objectified data	Difficult to rank a long list of items Distinctions are called for that are not perceived
	Semantic Differentials	Easy to complete Produces objectified data More difficult to give "socially acceptable" responses	Difficult to score

Figure 3 (Continued)

Information Collection Alternatives		Advantages	Disadvantages
Written Self-Report Measures (Cont.)	Q-Sorts	Produces objectified data Forces respondents to establish priorities among items	Distinctions are called for that are not perceived Directions can be too elaborate Can require complex data analysis method
	Diaries and Critical Incidents	Permits people to describe unique situations in their own words	People don't maintain them Difficult to score and interpret

Figure 3 (Continued)

The purpose of a field test is to answer questions such as:

- Will the instruments provide the needed information? Are certain words or questions redundant or misleading? Are the instruments appropriate for the people you will be testing?

- Will information collectors be able to use the instruments properly? Can they administer, collect, and report information using the written directions and special coding forms?

- Are the procedures standardized? Is everyone collecting information the same way?

- How consistent is the information obtained by the instruments? (Is it reliable?)

- How accurate is the information obtained with the instruments? (Is it valid?)

Field testing means trying out the instruments under conditions similar to those you expect to have for the evaluation, so you should involve a representative sample of people who will participate in the evaluation.

The nature and scope of a field test can vary considerably. Sometimes very formal field tests are required, and field test sites are prearranged by the sponsors of the program or the sponsor of the evaluation. If the details of field testing are not stipulated, however, it's usually up to the evaluator to find a site and test the information collection instruments.

Even though a thorough field test may not always be possible, you should be as systematic as you can within the limits imposed by time and money. Whenever feasible, use the same sampling plan you will use for the evaluation to select a minisample for the field test. (Remember that individuals, families, professionals, and others who participate in the field test shouldn't be included in the later evaluation because they will be familiar with the evaluation measures—a threat to the internal validity of the evaluation design.)

No matter how complete a field test might be, there's always a chance that it won't uncover all the problems you might encounter with information collection. Therefore, it's a good idea to ask some experts to review the evaluation instruments and any accompanying instructions about how to use them. These experts should be familiar with the program and its subject area, understand psychometrics, and know enough about information collection to help identify and solve potential problems.

Results of the field test may indicate the need to revise the information collection instruments. Depending on the extent of the revisions, you should repeat field testing until you're sure that the instruments are feasible and produce credible information.

Two factors that must always be taken into account when validating evaluation instruments are reliability and validity. An instrument is reliable if it provides consistent measurements, and it is valid if it provides accurate and relevant information.

How to Establish Reliability

A ruler is considered to be a reliable instrument if it yields the same result every time it's used to measure the same object, assuming the object itself hasn't changed. Similarly, an attitude questionnaire is considered reliable if the results are consistent each time the same person completes it, again assuming the person hasn't changed.

People do change, of course. You may be more tired, angry, and tense today than you were yesterday. People also change because of their experiences or because they learn something new, but meaningful changes are not subject to random fluctuations. A reliable instrument will provide a consistent measure of important characteristics despite background fluctuations. Three major types of reliability are stability, equivalence, and homogeneity.

First, does the instrument have stability? One way to estimate reliability is to see whether someone taking the same test performs about the same on more than one occasion. Stability is usually computed by administering an instrument to the same group on two different occasions and then correlating the scores from one time to the next. This type of reliability is also known as *test/retest reliability*. An instrument is considered reliable if the correlation between scores is high; that is, people who score high (or low) on the first occasion also score high (or low) on the second occasion.

Stability is probably the most important index of an instrument's reliability. Don't use instruments unless they have satisfactory test/retest correlation coefficients. For knowledge tests, correlations of .90 or higher are generally considered good enough. There's less agreement about what's acceptable for affective measures, but you can probably use instruments with correlations of .75 or better without criticism from measurement experts.

Second, are alternate forms equivalent? If two different forms of an instrument are supposed to appraise the same skills, knowledge, or attitudes, you have to make sure that people will score the same regardless of which form they take. If you want to use Form A of an instrument for a premeasure and Form B for a postmeasure, for example, check the equivalence of the two forms to make sure that one is not more difficult than the other.

Equivalence reliability can be computed by giving two or more forms of an instrument to the same group of people on the same day, or by giving different forms of the instrument to two or more groups that have been randomly selected.

Equivalence is determined by comparing the mean score and standard deviation of each form of the instrument and by correlating the scores on each form with the scores on the others. If the various forms have almost the same means and standard deviations and if they are highly correlated, then they have high equivalence reliability. Reliability coefficients of .90 or above on alternate forms are generally considered good.

Third, does the instrument have homogeneity? Is it internally consistent? Another measure of the reliability is how well all the items or questions on an instrument assess the same skill, characteristics, or quality. This type of reliability is called homogeneity or internal consistency. You should be especially concerned about homogeneity if you are using an instrument to measure a single skill, concept, or construct (pain or perceived physician skill, for example), or if the instrument is divided into several parts, each of which is supposed to measure a separate concept or skill.

To test for homogeneity, divide the instrument or subscale into two equal parts and correlate the scores on one half with the scores on the other half. This procedure is called *split-half reliability*, and it estimates whether both halves of the instrument measure the same skills and characteristics. Another way to estimate an instrument's homogeneity is by using the Kuder-Richardson Formula-20, also called coefficient alpha. This formula is really the average score obtained from computing all possible split-half reliabilities.

How to Establish Validity

A ruler is considered to be a valid instrument if it provides an accurate measure of a person's height. A rating scale applied to videotapes of sessions between psychiatric residents and patients is considered valid if it provides an accurate measure of residents' interviewing skill. A valid instrument is always a reliable one, but a reliable instrument is not always valid.

If you develop an instrument that consists of nothing more than asking a hospital administrator how many beds are in a given ward, for example, and you get the same answer on at least two occasions, you would have an instrument with test/retest reliability. But if you claim that the same instrument will measure the quality of medical care, you have a reliable instrument of questionable validity. Evaluation instruments that are valid must first be reliable, but instruments that are reliable are not necessarily valid. Four common types of validity are predictive, concurrent, content, and construct.

Does it have predictive validity? You can validate an instrument by proving that it predicts an individual's ability to perform a given task or behave in a certain way. For example, a medical school entrance examination has predictive validity if it accurately forecasts performance in medical school. One way of establishing predictive validity is to administer the instrument to all students wishing to enter medical school, and then to compare those scores with their performance in school. If the two sets of scores show a high positive or negative correlation, the instrument has predictive validity.

Does it have concurrent validity? You can validate an instrument by comparing it against a known and accepted measure. To establish concurrent validity of a new test of mathematical knowledge, you could administer the new test and an already established, validated measure to the same group of examinees and compare the scores from both instruments, or you could administer just the new test to the examinees and compare their scores on it to experts' judgments of subjects' knowledge. A high correlation between the new test and the criterion measure (the established test or experts' judgments) means concurrent validity. Remember, a concurrent validity study is only valuable if the criterion measure is convincing.

Does it have content validity? An instrument can be validated by proving that its items or questions accurately represent the skills or characteristics that they are intended to measure. A test of pharmacological vocabulary has content validity, for example, if it contains a reasonable sample of words commonly used in biochemical literature or recognized by pharmacologists. Content validity is usually established by asking experts whether the items are a representative sample of the skills and traits you want to measure.

Does it have construct validity? An instrument can be validated by demonstrating that it measures a psychological construct such as hostility or satisfaction. Construct validity is established experimentally by trying out the instrument on people who the experts say exhibit the behaviors associated with the construct. If people who have high degrees of hostility or satisfaction also obtain high scores on instruments designed to measure hostility or satisfaction, the instruments are considered to have construct validity.

HOW TO COLLECT ACCURATE DATA
IN THE FIELD

Selecting an evaluation design, developing instruments, and analyzing data are often considered the most technically difficult aspects of an evaluation. Logistically, however, information collection can be even more complicated. Here are some suggestions for getting accurate and complete evaluation data:

How to Hire Information Collectors

An information collection plan usually specifies the instruments that will be used to obtain information and the times when and locations at which each will be administered, but it often fails to specify the people who will supervise and perform collection. A plan may say that the evaluation team will mail questionnaires to the program's participants, for example, but it may not list the names of those who will be responsible for obtaining questionnaire forms, buying envelopes and stamps, and seeing that the mail goes out. Before you can begin collecting information, you must select the information collection staff.

You can use members of your evaluation staff, professional data collection agencies, or laypersons to collect information. A major advantage of relying on the evaluation staff is the control you have over information collection. Another advantage is that direct participation may help you understand the program's dynamics and impact.

Information collection usually takes a great deal of time, however, and you should ask yourself whether it's efficient to use your own staff during peak information collection periods. For instance, a three-member evaluation team based in New York would find it too expensive and physically exhausting to administer personally questionnaires in twenty cities within a 3-week period. Fortunately, professional data collection agencies are available to help, although their staffs are not always well trained and they are usually not subject to your instruction.

Sometimes you can hire people who are not affiliated with any special organization (like the residents of a community in which a program is being tried) to collect evaluation information as needed. Such people are relatively inexpensive to use, but they have no particular interest in the evaluation and little or no experience in collecting information and, they must, therefore, be trained.

The best way to find professional information collectors is to look in the classified sections of professional journals. Personal referrals are also helpful. To find information collectors with no formal organizational affiliation, try the faculty and students of local high schools and colleges, employment and social action agencies, and advertisements.

You can draw up a set of criteria to give employment agencies as a guide. Here's an example of some criteria for finding and choosing information collectors for an evaluation of a health education program:

Example 54   Criteria for Selecting Information Collectors

Preference for the job of field evaluator should be given to people with:

- a current valid driver's license
- at least a BA or BS degree
- credits in nursing, public health, social work, or teaching
- experience in a hospital, social agency, or school
- sound and practical judgment
- interpersonal skills
- the ability to follow directions

When selecting the information collection staff, be sure to consider these factors:

Availability. Select people who can be there when you need them to collect information. If interviews must be conducted during the day, you must choose people who are available then. Sometimes you will have to work with their employers to establish availability. Don't count on nurses with night duty to conduct noon interviews, for instance.

Special hiring requirements. Many evaluations are funded by local, state, or federal agencies, all of which are subject to civil rights and equal opportunity laws. These laws may affect who you can hire and how quickly you can hire them. Affirmative action, for example, requires a waiting period during which any interested person can apply for the available position.

Bias. The personalities and attitudes of the information collectors can have a substantial impact on the amount, quality, and accuracy of the information they collect. Sometimes local people can obtain more candid and valid information from their own community than college professors can, for example.

How to Train Information Collectors

Since most people don't have the technical skills needed in information collection, training is usually necessary. All training programs for information collectors should include certain basic themes. Trainees should learn something about the program, the evaluation questions, and the specific job they will be doing. In addition, you should make sure they get detailed instructions about how to obtain, record, and communicate information. To do this, give trainees a chance to:

- review the information collection instruments,
- practice administering the instruments,
- practice recording the information they get,
- learn how to report information to you or your staff, and
- learn how to deal with potential problems.

It's also very helpful to give trainees a guide to information collection. This can be a packet containing copies of all instruments and forms, directions for administering and collecting information, names of people to contact and places to visit during information collection, names of people on your staff to contact in case of trouble, and a list of possible problems and solutions.

The following example is part of the problem/solution list for information collectors in an evaluation of an education program.

Example 55   Problem/Solution List for Information Collectors

Program: An education program for elementary schoolchildren.

Problem: You can't collect the required number of questionnaires because some teachers haven't completed them.

Solution: Try to convince school officials that it's important to obtain the information on as many children as possible. Point out that the legislature will make funding decisions on the basis of what you find. If the school is willing, have the staff mail you the forms. Provide a label for the manila envelope if necessary.

How to Start Collecting Information

Obtain clearance. Most information collection activities are subject to legal restrictions on who is eligible to obtain information and the kinds of information you can collect. As a result, the instruments and procedures usually must receive clearance. For example, the Office of Management and Budget (OMB) is responsible for clearing information activities used in federally sponsored evaluations.

When confronted with clearance requirements, it's a good idea to ask for help from a program official or your evaluation sponsor. The steps involved in obtaining clearance may take many months, with long intervals between submission of drafts. You must organize the information collection schedule so that you will have enough time to obtain the necessary authorizations.

Inform participants. Information collection involves many people, and it's your job to explain what you want them to do and why. You can hold a meeting or a workshop or you can rely on the mail or telephone. Be sure to have a written description of the program as well as the evaluation and its information collection activities for anyone who wants to see it. Finally, don't forget to thank participants and tell them what their participation meant to the project.

Monitor information collection. Carefully monitor information collection to see that it is going according to plan and that all relevant data are being collected and returned. You can do this in several ways. You can have one person on the evaluation staff take the responsibility for monitoring activities, or you can have two people collect identical information independently and compare the results for reliability. Check information as it is returned to determine whether it was collected according to plan, and whether there are any unexpected findings or violations of confidentiality.

How to Organize Evaluation Information for Analysis

Information collected during an evaluation is frequently returned in a form that can't be analyzed immediately. Tests may have to be scored or interview responses may need to be coded and tallied. Since information is usually collected at different times, you will have to coordinate it so that a complete set is eventually available.

Most evaluations involve gathering large amounts of data that can become unmanageable unless you find a way to organize them. Even a brief 2-page questionnaire with 25 items completed by 300 people generates 600 pieces of paper and 7500 bits of information. Remember, the ease with which you can answer evaluation questions depends upon how well you organize the information collected.

Consider an evaluation question that asks whether patients' percep-tions of their health care providers are related to their health status. If you asked patients whether their doctors like them or not and then categorize their answers as "sometimes," "yes," "s/he thinks I'm okay," "I don't like him/her," it would be very difficult to answer the question. If, instead, you categorize patients' responses to the same question on a scale such as "definitely yes," "probably yes," "not sure," "probably not," "definitely not," then you can answer the question more easily. Organizing the information for analysis can become a major activity requiring careful planning and considerable time. Usually it means categorizing free response data, assigning codes when computer analyses are planned, and rostering data.

To organize evaluation information collected from open-ended questions, the responses must be categorized. You can do this by developing categories in advance and then placing responses in the right slots, or you can do it by developing the categories after you sift through the data.

Suppose you asked, "What parts of your continuing education program were most useful?" If 180 out of 300 people mentioned lectures and only two mentioned films and readings, then "lectures" would probably be considered one distinct category. Films and readings would fall under a second category, perhaps labeled "other." If you had set the categories in advance, then lectures, films, and readings might have been considered separate and equal parts of the continuing education program.

Coding is the process of assigning a numerical value to each piece of information. Numerical codes are just names for data that are shorter than words and therefore easier to record, store, analyze, and retrieve. Usually codes are only assigned to information that is going to be analyzed by a computer.

Example 56   Sample Coding Directions

Information	Codes	Column(s)
(1) Participant's Name	001 to 999, in alphabetical order	1-3
(2) Participant's Sex	1 – Male 2 – Female 3 – No data	4
(3) Participant's Educational Background	1 – Some high school 2 – High school graduate 3 – Some college 4 – College graduate 5 – Professional or graduate training 9 – No data	5
(4) Pretest Score	Keypunch total score (0-10)	6-7
(5) Posttest Items 1-10	For each multiple choice item, 1 – A 2 – B 3 – C 4 – D 9 – No data	8-17
(6) Posttest Score	Keypunch total score (0-10)	18-19

It's possible to assign codes to any kind of evaluation information, such as participant's name, sex, educational background, and geographic location. The choice of which number represents a category of information is arbitrary. Usually, consecutive numbers are chosen and one number (typically the highest) is reserved for an "other" or "no data" category. In addition, the coding process often involves identifying the places on a computer card where the codes will be recorded by keypunchers. Sample coding directions are presented in Example 56.

To roster information, you must identify all the different pieces of data that have been collected and then list them for each individual or group. For example, information from a demographic questionnaire survey of patients, pretest and posttest scores, interviews with hospital administrators, and a review of hospital financial records might be rostered as in Examples 57a and 57b. (Note that the information has been

Example 57a Rostering Evaluation Information: Participation Level

Name	Sex	Education	Pretest Total	Item 1	Item 2	Item 3	Item 4	Item 5	Item 6	Item 7	Item 8	Item 9	Item 10	Posttest Total
0 0 1	1	4	0 2	1	2	3	1	4	9	1	4	2	2	0 3
0 0 2	1	2	0 4	9	2	2	2	1	4	3	2	2	9	0 5
0 0 3	1	2	0 5	1	2	2	2	3	2	4	4	4	9	0 4
0 0 4	2	3	0 3	2	2	2	2	2	9	4	3	2	1	0 6
0 0 5	2	9	0 5	1	2	3	4	9	2	2	2	2	2	0 6
0 0 6	1	5	0 4	2	2	2	2	9	1	2	3	3	3	0 5
0 0 7	2	1	0 3	1	3	4	9	1	2	2	2	2	2	0 5
0 0 8	2	9	0 5	2	2	2	3	9	2	9	9	9	2	0 5
0 0 9	2	1	0 5	2	2	2	2	2	1	2	2	2	2	0 9
0 1 0	1	3	0 2	1	1	1	1	3	9	3	1	2	2	0 2

organized at two levels: the patient—individual participant—and the hospital—institution.)

HOW TO DESIGN ACHIEVEMENT TESTS

Regardless of the types of programs you evaluate, you frequently will want to ask questions about knowledge: How much is learned, by

Example 57b Rostering Evaluation Information: Institution Level

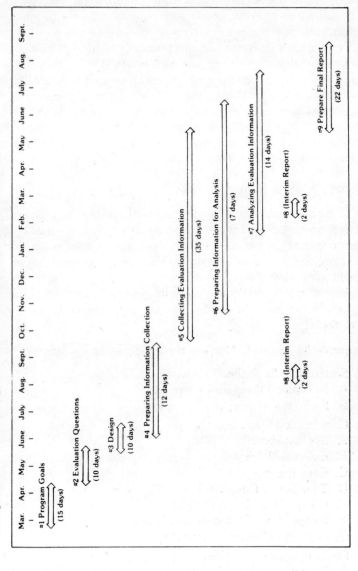

*The numbers in the parentheses refer to the amount of professional staff time allocated to each activity.

131

whom, and how efficiently? Achievement information is usually collected with paper-and-pencil tests administered before a program and immediately after, or even much later.

Existing tests to assess knowledge are not always available, and the evaluator may have to design these measures. To do this, you should first prepare a content/process matrix. The matrix is a table that matches a program's subject matter to the knowledge and skills that should be learned. Evaluators use it to decide which objectives to test and how students should demonstrate their knowledge and skills. Always develop a content/process matrix before you begin writing achievement measures. Here's how to do it.

Identify Subject Matter (Content)

To plan an achievement test, you must first have an outline of the subject matter or content of the program. A test needn't measure every objective or subject area covered in a program or course. By carefully selecting topics and measuring each in appropriate detail, you can obtain an estimate of an individual's general knowledge or achievement. Keep the outline brief by using only general categories of subject matter. Here's an example of a subject matter outline for a course in evaluation.

Example 58   Sample Outline for a Course in Evaluation

  I. Formulating Evaluation Questions
     A. Evaluator's Program Description
     B. Evaluation Questions
 II. Constructing Evaluation Design
     A. Internal Validity
     B. External Validity
     C. Case Designs
     D. Time-Series Designs
     E. Comparison Group Designs
     F. Independent and Dependent Variables
     G. Evaluation Design Description
III. Planning Information Collection
     A. Techniques Used to Collect Information
     B. Selecting, Adapting, or Developing the Right Instrument for Information Collection
     C. Preparing Information Collection Forms

Identify Learning Outcomes (Process)

The second step in achievement test planning is to define the outcomes of learning in specific terms. Learning outcomes differ from subject matter areas because they tell what examinees should be able to do to demonstrate their knowledge and skills.

Suppose, for example, an evaluator wants to know whether individuals are familiar with information collection techniques. Since the words *familiar with* could mean being able to recognize techniques, understand principles, or know when to use one technique instead of another, you must be very specific about which behavior the learner should demonstrate.

On the whole, it's better to state learning outcomes as observable or measurable behaviors. Here are some words to use for stating outcomes:

recognizes	describes
identifies	gives an example
distinguishes between	explains
selects	predicts

Most learning outcomes can be grouped into four categories: knowledge and skills, attitudes, interests, and appreciations. Achievement tests are most useful for measuring knowledge and skills. Other kinds of learning are more easily assessed by rating scales, checklists, and inventories.

Bloom (1956) described levels of knowledge, intellectual skills, and abilities in his famous monograph as consisting of knowledge (recall of already learned material), comprehension (understanding facts and principles), application (the ability to use knowledge in specific cases), analysis (the ability to divide knowledge into its component parts), synthesis (the ability to bring component parts together), and evaluation (using standards to determine the appropriateness of facts or theories in certain situations).

Prepare a Content/Process Matrix

The third step in achievement test planning is to actually prepare a content/process matrix describing the relationship between subject matter and observable behaviors and specifying the number of test items for each subject area and learning outcome.

Example 59   Sample Content/Process Matrix for a Test on Reliability and Validity

Process (Outcome)	Content (Subject Area)			Total Number of Items
	What is Reliability?	What is Validity?	Evaluating Tests	
Defines Terms	2	4	0	6
Gives Examples	3	5	0	8
Understands Principles	3	5	0	8
Interprets Statistical Indices	2	5	0	7
Computes Statistical Indices	2	4	0	6
Selects Best Alternatives	0	0	10	10
Total Number of Items	12	23	10	45

In Example 59, you will see a simple matrix. The number in each cell indicates the number of test items to be included for a particular area/process combination. Twelve items in the test, for example, will measure the student's knowledge of reliability, and two of those twelve will ask the student to define terms. Notice that the number of items assigned to each cell varies according to the importance given to the subject matter area and the behavior. Decisions about what is important should reflect the program's philosophy. It's a good idea to consult the developers or other sponsors to be sure you have the right priorities.

One final thing to consider is the total number of items on an achievement test. On the whole, long tests provide the best sample of achievement, contain the least amount of error, and have the highest test/retest reliability.

Selecting Item Types

When you construct an achievement test to fit a table of specifications like the one in Example 59, you will have a variety of item types from which to choose. Objective items are generally used to measure cognitive learning because they can be easily adapted to specific lessons, provide an adequate sample of individual performance, and be scored quickly and objectively. Objective items include items that require the test takers to select an answer, i.e., multiple-choice, true/false, and matching. They also include items for which the test taker must supply short answers.

Essay questions are considered subjective because their scoring involves personal judgment. Essay questions are rarely used in evaluations, but they can be valuable when the importance of getting a creative response outweighs difficulties in scoring.

When should you use multiple-choice items? Multiple-choice items consist of a problem and several possible solutions. They are considered best for evaluations because they can be used to measure almost all types and levels of learning. They are very easy to score, and a set of sophisticated procedures has been developed for establishing how accurately and consistently they measure achievement.

If you are measuring knowledge of facts, methods, specific theories, or principles, you will find multiple-choice questions relatively easy to construct. It's much harder to produce multiple-choice items that measure higher-level intellectual abilities such as analyzing relationships or making judgments based on external criteria. Here are some examples of multiple-choice items:

Example 60   Multiple-Choice Items

The manic attempts to maintain ego integrity by which of the following means?

_____A. repressive mechanisms primarily
_____B. intropunitive reactions that relieve guilt feelings
_____C. projection of the blame for difficulties onto enemies
__x__D. denial of sense of inadequacy by playing role of increased self-esteem
_____E. marked hyperactivity to overcome underlying basic passivity

Children who cannot read by the fourth grade are most often:

_____A. mentally retarded
__x__B. culturally disadvantaged
_____C. brain damaged
_____D. suffering a major perceptual handicap

When should you use true/false items? The true/false item should be used when there are only two possible solutions to a problem. If you want to know whether examinees can distinguish facts from opinions or tell whether a given agreement is relevant or irrelevant, then true/false items are appropriate.

Contrary to popular belief, this is one of the most difficult kinds of items to construct. It calls for unqualified judgments of truth or falsity, but in most areas of knowledge, important statements must be qualified. What's more, the uninformed person has a 50-50 chance of guessing the answer. Finally, knowing that something is false doesn't always mean that you know what's true. Examples of true-false items are:

(x)T ( )F   True/false questions use objective scoring systems.

( )T (x)F   The polio vaccine also provides immunity against distemper.

When should you use matching items? The matching item is a modification of the multiple-choice form in which a series of problems is listed in one column and the responses are listed in another. This item type is relatively difficult to construct because its usefulness depends on having all the responses serve as plausible solutions.

The matching item is very well suited to testing materials presented in pictorial form. You can ask examinees to match a series of entries on a graph or a set of closely related pictures (e.g., roentgenograms, electrocardiograms) with a list of statements about them.

The following is an example of a matching item:

Example 61 Item Matching

Column I describes the history of various mental health acts and Column II gives the names of health legislation. Match the descriptors with the names of legislation by placing the letter corresponding the legislation's title in Column II to the left of each descriptor in Column I. Each lettered entry in Column II may be selected once, more than once, or not at all.

Column I	Column II
_____ 1. Established the Joint Commission on Mental Illness and Health	A. Mental Health Study Act B. Mental Retardation Facilities and community Health Centers Act

_____2. Passed by Congress in 1963

_____3. Authorized the appropriation of more than $100,000,000 for research and treatment facilities for the mentally retarded

_____4. Authorized the appropriation of funds to finance the total construction costs of community mental health centers

C. National Mental Health Act

D. Comprehensive Health Planning Act

E. Social Security: Disability Insurance Act

(answers: 1-A, 2-B, 3-B, 4-D)

When should you use completion items? The short-answer or completion item is the only objective item type that requires supplying rather than selecting an answer. It consists of a question or incomplete statement that requires the test taker to fill in appropriate words, numbers, or symbols.

Since it's difficult to phrase questions or statements so that only one answer is correct, short-answer items tend to be useful only in tests that call for memorizing and recalling knowledge. Here are examples of completion items:

---

1. In the Problem Oriented Medical Record (POMR) system, the letters S-O-A-P are abbrevations for what words?

   _____ , _____ , _____ , _____

2. The major blood vessel leading from the heart to the stomach is the_____ artery.

Answers: 1—subjective/objective/assessment/plan
          2—celiac

When should you use essay items? The essay item requires a unique answer and allows the test taker to decide how to approach a problem, what factual information to use, how to organize a reply, and how much emphasis to give each aspect of the answer. The essay item is most useful for evaluating the ability to produce, integrate, and express ideas. Its limitations include the relatively small sampling of achievement it provides (since only a small number of essay items can be used at any one time) and the difficulty of establishing scoring standards.

The amount of freedom permitted by essay items varies. Examinees may be asked to give a brief and precisely defined response (restricted response) or they may be given much freedom in determining the nature and scope of their answer (extended response).

Here are examples of restricted and extended essay items:

Restricted Essay	*Extended Essay*
Describe two types of measurement validity.	Discuss the value of chemotherapy in treating gastric carcinomas.
Choose one member institute of the NIH and describe this agency's major responsibilities.	Explain the economic consequences of the XYZ national health insurance program.

The characteristics and the limitations of the various item types are summarized in Figures 4 and 5.

HOW TO CONSTRUCT MULTIPLE-CHOICE ITEMS

Multiple-choice items play an important role in the objective assessment of knowledge, opinions, and feelings. Many evaluators advocate the use of multiple-choice items because they have a wider range of uses than types such as true/false, they can measure a wider sample of performance than essay items, and they are objective and easy to score. For these reasons, multiple-choice items are commonly found in knowledge tests as well as in opinion questionnaire surveys.

The multiple-choice item consists of a stem, which presents a problem (typically in the form of a statement, a question, a brief case history, or a situation), followed by several alternative choices or solutions. The choices (usually four or five in all) include distracters.

	Construction	Scoring	Use	Comments
Multiple Choice	Easy to construct for relatively low levels of achievement, e.g., recall of facts; much more difficult for higher levels, e.g., analysis	Objective	For most all levels of achievement: very flexible	Frequently used by evaluators
True/False	Very difficult	Objective	Only when a statement is unquestionably true or false: inflexible	
Matching	Difficult	Objective	When only one or a few words will answer question: inflexible	
Short Answer (Completion)	Easy	Relatively Objective	When only one or a few words will answer a question: inflexible	
Essay	Relatively Easy	Subjective	When judging ability to produce, integrate, express ideas	Rarely used by evaluators

Figure 4   Characteristics of Item Types

The purpose of the distracters is to tease the test taker by appearing to be correct.

Here are examples of the two major kinds of multiple choice items, the question form and the incomplete statement form:

Example 62   Multiple-Choice Items

Question Form
Who is called the father of psychoanalysis?
- A. Carl Jung
- B. Erik Erikson
- *C. Sigmund Freud
- D. Eric Fromm
- E. Harry Stack Sullivan

	Advantages	Limitations
Multiple Choice	Useful for measuring many levels of achievement Easy to score	Cannot measure the expression, production, or integration of ideas
True/False	Useful for distinguishing fact from opinion, the relevant from the inappropriate Easy to score	Difficult to construct Cannot be used to measure the higher levels of achievement
Matching	Easy to score	Limited to situations in which many plausible alternatives exist
Short Answer (Completion)	Relatively easy to construct	Restricted to situations in which just one or a few words can answer a question
Essay	Relatively easy to construct The only way to measure the expression, production, and integration of ideas	Difficult to score

Figure 5   Advantages and Limitations of Item Types

Incomplete Answer Form

The father of psychoanalysis is:
A. Carl Jung
B. Erik Erikson
*C. Sigmund Freud
D. Eric Fromm
E. Harry Stack Sullivan

From these examples, you can see that the incomplete statement is more concise than the question. Although the question form is usually easier to write, it often results in a longer stem.

Another type of multiple-choice item is the best answer form. Unlike the question or statement form, in which only one answer is clearly correct, the best-answer has alternatives that are all partially correct but one is clearly better than the others. This format is used for evaluating complex achievement such as the ability to select the best course of action or the best method or example.

Example 63   Best Answer Form

In general, a first case of German measles is most serious for

    A. babies 8 months to 18 months.
    B. girls 13-18 years of age.
  *C. women who are pregnant.
    D. adult males 65 years or older.

To avoid confusion, always specify whether the test taker is to select the correct or the best answer.

No matter what type of multiple-choice item you use, be sure to include four or five distracters to choose from. With four alternatives, there is one chance in four that an item will be answered correctly because the examinee made the right guess. With five alternatives the chance is one in five. In order to correct for guessing, however, all items must have the same number of distracters. Gronlund (1977) recommends the following correction-for-guessing formula:

$$\text{Score} = \text{Right} - \text{Wrong}/n - 1$$

n = number of distracters

Here are some rules for writing multiple-choice items.

Rule 1: Design each item to measure an important learning outcome. Make sure that items measure only what the program is designed to achieve. If a program is supposed to teach students to select appropriate statistical techniques, don't depend on items asking for the recall of statistical formulas or the computation of statistics.

Rule 2: Present a single, clearly formulated problem in the stem of the item. The problem in the stem should be stated so clearly that you can answer it without reading the choices. Try these ideas:

Example 64   Multiple-Choice Problems

Poor: Multiple-choice items
A. are frequently used to make essay tests more objective.
B. were invented for use in intelligence testing.
C. are scored objectively in contrast to matching items.
*D. can be used to measure knowledge, opinions, or feelings.

Better: What is the main advantage of using multiple choice items
rather than essay items for evaluations?
*A. They can be scored more quickly and objectively.
B. They are best for measuring complex learning outcomes.
C. They can have more than one right answer.
D. They are the least threatening of the item types.

Rule 3: State the stem of the item in simple, clear language. Unnecessary or obscure words may confuse people who actually know the correct answer. Using too many words makes the test taker spend unnecessary time reading the item rather than responding to it. Wordy items are apt to test overall reading ability rather than intended learning outcomes.

Example 65   Wordiness

Poor: The paucity of psychometric scales with high degrees of
stability and construct validity is most bothersome to evaluators when assessing people's
A. characteristics.
*B. feelings.
C. knowledge.
D. health.

Better: The lack of reliable and valid instruments causes evaluators
the most problems when measuring people's
A. characteristics.
*B. feelings.
C. knowledge.
D. health.

Poor: Since 1960, most federally sponsored programs include
mandates for evaluation in the legislation that created the
program. However, one federal program that has *no* evaluation requirements is:

Better: One federal program that has *no* evaluation requirements in
                its legislation is:

Rule 4: Put as much of the wording in the stem as possible. Avoid
repeating the same words in the distracters that you use in the stem.
Look at these items:

Example 66 Word Use

Poor: To most health professionals the abbreviation JAMA
                A. stands for Joint Association on Medical Accreditation.
              *B. stands for the *Journal of the American Medical
                   Association.*
                C. stands for *Journal of the Academy of Medical
                   Abstractors.*
                D. stands for Joint Alliance of Medicine and the Arts.

Better: To most health professionals the abbreviation JAMA stands
                for
                A. Joint Association on Medical Accreditation.
              *B. *Journal of the American Medical Association.*
                C. *Journal of the Academy of Medical Abstractors.*
                D. Joint Alliance of Medicine and the Arts.

Rule 5: State the stem of the item in positive form wherever possible.
Most learning focuses on the best method or the most supporting data
and not on the poorest or the least supporting. If you ask questions that
concentrate on the negative, you are asking people to remember
incorrect information. Remember that being able to identify an
incorrect approach or provide a negative opinion doesn't necessarily
mean that someone can choose the correct approach or offer a valid,
positive opinion.

Example 67 Focusing on the Most Supporting Data

Poor: Which of the following is *not* a hormone secreted by the
                pituitary?
                A. thyrotropic hormone
                B. growth hormone
              *C. epinephrine
                D. prolactin

Better: Which of the following is a hormone secreted by the
pituitary?
A. thyroxin
*B. prolactin
C. progesterone
D. cortisol

Rule 6: Emphasize negative wording whenever it is used in the stem of an item. Sometimes it's necessary to use negatives in testing certain types of knowledge or attitudes. Knowing when not to play with fire might be one example important enough to warrant the use of negative words. When you use negatives, emphasize them with underlining or with capital letters and place them near the end of the statement. Try these items:

Example 68   Negatives

Poor: Competency-based tests are not appropriate for measuring
A. skills.
*B. opinions.
C. achievement.
D. knowledge.

Better: Competency-based tests are appropriate for measuring all
of the following except:
A. skills.
*B. opinions.
C. achievement.
D. knowledge.

Rule 7: Make sure that the intended answer is correct or clearly best. Multiple-choice items must have one answer that is unquestionably correct or best. You can use the phrase "of the following" in the stem of the item if there's another possible correct answer that is not given. It's also important to phrase the stem of an item so that a correct or best answer is readily apparent to the informed. For example:

Poor: What is the purpose of evaluation?

Better: One important purpose of evaluation is . . .

Rule 8: Make all alternatives grammatically consistent with the stem of the item and parallel in form. The correct or best answer must be grammatically consistent with the stem. This means that the tenses, articles, and syntax in the stem should be consistent with those in the distracters. As a general rule, you should avoid using an article at the end of the stem.

Example 69   Grammatical Consistency

Poor: In general, two categorical variables can best be compared with a
                 *A. chi-square test.
                  B. analysis of covariance.
                  C. descriptive statistics.
                  D. stepwise regression analyses.

Better: In general, two categorical variables can best be compared with
                 *A. chi-square tests.
                  B. analysis of covariance.
                  C. descriptive statistics.
                  D. stepwise regression analyses.

Rule 9: Avoid verbal clues. Don't repeat important words from the stem in the correct answer. Don't use synonyms or words that look alike in both the stem and the correct answer. Sometimes a testwise examinee will spot the correct answer just because it sounds technical or scholarly.

If you state the correct answer in greater detail than the incorrect ones, you're offering another verbal clue. This occurs when the test maker wants to be sure that the correct or best answer won't be misinterpreted or challenged.

Qualifying words such as *usually, generally, may,* and *typically* are also clues to the answer. Distracters that include absolutes such as *never, no one, everyone,* and *all* are clues because many test takers have learned that they appear often in incorrect answers.

If you offer two responses that are all-inclusive, examinees can reject the other distracters because one of the two must be correct. Avoid using two responses that have the same meaning. After all, if only one distracter can be correct then the two synonyms can be eliminated.

Here are some examples of items containing verbal clues. How would you correct them?

Example 70   Verbal Clues

Similar wording in the stem and correct answer

Poor:
Which of the following is the most significant risk factor for myocardial infarctions?

*A. a history of heart disease
 B. presence of polyps in the abdomen
 C. family history of anemia
 D. type "B" personality

Stating the correct answer in technical terms

Poor:
One important purpose of stating objectives is to

*A. define a program's goals in operational terms.
 B. provide a basis for program evaluation.
 C. give a foundation for determining a program's costs.
 D. place priorities on a program's purposes.

Stating the correct answer in more detail

Poor:
A broad definition of program evaluation is

*A. a set of procedures used to assess a program's merit and to provide information about its goals, activities, outcomes, and costs.
 B. a technique for comparing two or more innovative programs.
 C. a systematic method for prioritizing programs with social goals.
 D. to judge the value of a social program in numerical terms.

Rule 10: Make all distracters plausible and attractive to the uninformed or poorly prepared examinee. Here are some guidelines for plausibility:

(1) Rely on common misconceptions.
(2) Use words and language style examinees expect to find.
(3) Use "good sounding" words (*accurate, important*) in the distracters as well as in the correct answer.
(4) Use extraneous clues in the distracters such as *scientific* or *scholarly* terms.
(5) Make all distracters equal in length and complexity of thought.

Rule 11: Vary the relative length of the correct answer to eliminate length as a clue. The correct answer often tends to be longer because of the need to qualify statements to make them unequivocally correct.

Rule 12: Avoid using the alternative "all of the above" and use "none of the above" with care. "All of the above" permits a correct response with only partial information. Knowing there can be only one answer, examinees will choose "all of the above" if two of the distracters are correct. Examinees can reject "all of the above" if they know that at least one of the choices is incorrect.

"None of the above" can't be used with "best-answer" multiple-choice questions, since the distracters all have to be incorrect. A "none of the above" question may be measuring nothing more than the ability to infer incorrect answers.

Example 71   None of the Above

Poor: Which of the following can be used to judge the validity of a
               test designed to estimate future performance?
               A. Equivalence
               B. Construct validity
               C. Stability
               *D. None of the above

Better: Which of the following can be used to judge the validity of a
               test designed to estimate future performance?
               A. Equivalence
               B. Construct validity
               C. Stability
               *D. Predictive validity

Rule 13: Vary the position of the correct answer in a random manner. The correct answer should appear in each alternative position about the same number of times. Avoid using a pattern for placement of the correct answer.

Rule 14: Use an efficient item format. List the alternatives on separate lines to make them easier to read and compare. When writing an item, follow the conventional rules of grammar. For example, when the stem is an incomplete statement, each alternative should begin with a lowercase letter and end with the proper punctuation mark, usually a period. If distracters are complete sentences they should begin with capital letters and end with periods.

HOW TO USE QUESTIONNAIRES

Try this short quiz about questionnaires by checking which statements are generally true or false.

Statements	True	False
(1) Questionnaires can be a quick and inexpensive way to reach large numbers of people.	_____	_____
(2) Questionnaires are convenient for people to complete.	_____	_____
(3) Questionnaires can provide reliable and valid information.	_____	_____
(4) Questionnaires are easy to construct.	_____	_____
(5) Everyone likes questionnaires.	_____	_____

Questionnaires are a relatively inexpensive way to reach a large number of people quickly. Suppose, for example, that you want to find out whether subscribers are satisfied with a bulletin put out by the County Library Information Service. You might interview them in person or by phone, but it's often difficult to arrange interviews with people because their schedules don't coincide with yours or your staff's. Also, interviewers must be trained if they are to obtain reliable information, a costly and time-consuming process. Questionnaires— even when you take into account printing and mailing charges—cost considerably less than interviews to reach the same number of people.

Many people have become familiar with questionnaires and are accustomed to completing them. Mailed questionnaires may be particularly easy to complete, since people are under no pressure to finish all the questions within a certain amount of time.

Reliability and validity are two attributes that evaluators look for in all their instruments, including questionnaires. It helps to try out the questionnaire with a number of people before you send it out, just to make sure that the wording is clear and that you are likely to get consistently accurate information.

Constructing questionnaires is no easier than constructing other instruments and it requires many skills. The directions and the questions should be written clearly and be easy to read, complete, and return.

A major problem with questionnaires is that you may get a low and perhaps unrepresentative response rate. Some may be unable to read the questions; some may be tired of answering questions. Not everyone likes questionnaires, and your evaluation may be incomplete without their response, but there is virtually no data-gathering technique that someone won't object to.

Designing the Questionnaire

Suppose you want to find out how useful subscribers have found the *Cancer Information Service Bulletin.* Here are some questions you must answer:

- What do I need to ask?
- Whom should I ask?
- How much money and time do I have?
- What should the questionnaire look like?

Step 1: Asking the right questions. Your first step in designing questionnaires is to specify the purposes of the study as precisely as you can. In the subscriber survey, the overall purpose is to identify how useful the bulletin is to subscribers. But subscribers may be classified in many different ways: all readers, all doctors, oncologists and radiologists only, nurses, psychiatrists.

And what do you mean by useful? Does it mean—worthwhile in terms of its value as a reference; as a teaching tool; as a source of information about services for patients and families? The questionnaire designer must begin with well-formed evaluation questions. Consider this example:

Example 72   The Right Questions

As the evaluator of a program to coordinate several cancer information services, you surveyed subscribers to the monthly *Cancer Information Service Bulletin.* The purpose of the survey was to provide information to answer a series of evaluation questions. One of the evaluation questions was "How do health professionals and other readers like scientists and the public compare in using the *Bulletin* to find out about services for patients?" You designed a questionnaire that contained the following questions.

Which of the following best describes you?

_____ Administrator
_____ Dentist
_____ Epidemiologist/Social Scientist
_____ Nurse
_____ Physician
_____ Other (specify) _____

How often do you use the Bulletin to find out about services for patients and their families?

_____ Always
_____ Sometimes
_____ Never

These two questions allowed you to get data on how many respondents were health professionals, scientists, and members of the public, and then to compare how they use the *Bulletin* to find out about patient services.

Step 2: Asking the right people in the right way. Make sure that the people you ask to complete the questionnaire include only those who are likely to provide relevant information. In the evaluation of the *Cancer Information Service Bulletin*, you should review the list of subscribers to make sure they are all appropriate respondents. If you send the questionnaire to nursing students and none of the questions are intended for them, don't be surprised if you get misleading or even useless information. Knowing who to ask is just as important as knowing what to ask.

When selecting groups such as health professionals, scientists, and members of the public, you may want to select individuals within groups. In the *Bulletin* survey for example, you might decide to include all doctors and nurses, but sample only a limited number of other health professionals, scientists, and members of the public.

Step 3: Paying for the questionnaires and getting them back on time. Make sure that you have enough money to pay for all phases of questionnaire development and use. You will need money for paper and to print the questionnaires and any follow-up forms. If you mail them you must pay postage, and in some cases, return postage. Don't forget to take the cost of envelopes into account and the staff time it takes to do the mailing and supervise the follow ups. Set up a realistic schedule for printing, distributing, and following up on each questionnaire, and for keypunching the returned forms.

Step 4: The questionnaire's format. The wary evaluator always worries about the questionnaire's response rate. Besides choosing the right people and asking them the right questions, you should:

- Make the questionnaire as appealing as possible by keeping it short and easy to read.
- Number all questions and pages.
- Include directions. Keep them short.
- Make sure respondents know who is sending the questionnaire to them.
- Tell respondents how you will be using the information they provide.
- Distinguish questionnaires that are anonymous or confidential from those that are not.

Step 5: How to construct items. Writing good items is one of the most difficult aspects of questionnaire design. Questions can take several forms: open-ended or essay, dichotomous questions ("yes" or "no" questions), fill-in-the-blanks, ranking questions, and multiple choice.
Here are some guidelines for asking questions.

- Word the questions as simply as possible. This is not the time to impress people with your vocabulary or your knowledge of technical terms. In a questionnaire to school psychologists you might ask about the affective domain, but in one to parents, you should ask about the attitudes of children.
- Ask questions that call for only one answer. Consider the following:

  Poor: How reliable and valid is the XYZ Inventory of Vocational Aptitude?

  Better: How reliable is the XYZ Inventory of Vocational Aptitude?
             How valid is the XYZ Inventory of Vocational Aptitude?

Suppose the XYZ Inventory is reliable but not valid; what would the respondent do? Asking for too much information in a single question only serves to confuse people.

Choose words that are unambiguous. Words such as *several, a few*, and *typically* mean different things to different people.

Step 6: How to organize responses. Be sure the respondent knows where to record responses. Confusion can discourage people from completing the questionnaire. To avoid this, follow these guidelines:

(1) Provide a response category for every possible answer. If you leave out a choice, people may give you invalid data.

Poor: Does your residence have forced air heating?

_____ Yes

_____ No

Better: Does your residence have forced air heating?

_____ Yes

_____ No

_____ Don't know

If people don't know what kind of heating is in their home they might guess. "Don't know" gives them an opportunity to provide a truthful answer.

(2) Keep response options independent of one another so that choosing one response is possible. How would you answer the following?

Poor: Which of the following are you?

_____ A nurse

_____ An administrator

_____ A medical records librarian

_____ A teacher

You could be a nurse and an administrator, a nurse and a teacher, and so on. A better version of a similar item would be:

Better: Which one of the following best describes your job?

_____ Nurse

_____ Administrator

_____ Medical records librarian

_____ Teacher

_____ Other

(3) Place responses vertically rather than horizontally.

Poor: _____ Yes   _____ No

Better: _____ Yes

_____ No

The problem with the horizontal placement is that respondents may be unsure of which line is the correct one to check for "yes."

(4) Keep scales balanced so that there are an equal number of degree of choices.

Good: Strongly agree
Agree
Neutral
Disagree
Strongly disagree

Good: Always
Frequently
Sometimes
Never

(5) Make sure the respondent can tell precisely what information is needed.

Poor: Where were you born?

Better: In what state or foreign country were you born?

Make sure the meaning of the words you use and the way you use them are generally accepted as the same by nearly everyone. People often disagree about the meaning of words such as *liberal, conservative, fair,* and the like. Take these examples from President Carter's Cabinet Staff Evaluation form:

Poor: How mature is the person?

1	2	3	4	5	6
immature					mature

Poor: How stable is this person?

1	2	3	4	5	6
erratic					steady

Poor: How confident is this person? (Circle one)

X	X	X	X	X	X
self-doubting		confident		cocky	

To get useful information about maturity, stability, or confidence, it would have been better to define the terms and to describe a situation that might test the qualities you are seeking. To estimate confidence, for example, you might ask:

Better: How confident is this person when asked to give a speech in front of a large audience?

1	2	3	4	5	6
very confident					not very confident

Scale: *very confident*—expresses ideas clearly and concisely; voice is clear; does not shuffle papers

not very confident—has difficulty expressing ideas; voice trembles; moves papers around

Note also that the original scale is probably not balanced because the opposite of self-doubting is not cocky. If the raters want to know whether the individual being rated is arrogant, they should devise a scale for that term.

Using the Questionnaire

Be sure to pilot test all questionnaires before they are distributed. If you use people who are representative of the group to be surveyed, you will find out whether the questionnaire is easy to use, read, and answer. Colleagues who have been involved in designing surveys and other experts should also be consulted to get the bugs out.

How to Boost the Response Rate

A major problem with questionnaires is that some people won't respond. Here's what you might do, depending on your needs and resources, to encourage responses:

- Send respondents a pre-letter telling them the purpose of your evaluation and of the questionnaire. Explain why the respondents should answer your questions, and tell them about others who are being surveyed.

- Prepare a short cover letter to accompany the questionnaire form. If you have already sent a pre-letter, this one should be very concise. It should again describe the study and questionnaire aims and participants.

- Offer to send respondents a summary of the findings so that they can see just how the data were used. (If you promise this, budget for it!)

- If you ask questions that may be construed as personal, such as sex, age, or income, explain why they are necessary.

- Keep questionnaire procedures simple. Provide stamped self-addressed envelopes. Keep paper folding to a minimum so respondents don't feel that they are involved in complicated psychomotor activities.

- Keep questionnaires as short as you can. Ask only the questions you are sure you need for the evaluation, and don't crowd them

together. Give participants enough room to write and be sure each
question is set apart from the next.

- Consider incentives. Gifts may encourage people to respond.
  These may range from money to pens or food.

- Be prepared to follow up or send reminders. These should be brief
  and to the point. It often helps to send another copy of the questionnaire. (Don't forget to budget money and time for these additional copies and mailing!)

HOW TO USE INTERVIEWS

An interview is a conversation (face-to-face or on the phone) in which
one person tries to obtain information from another. As an evaluator,
you may want to use interviews to learn more about the people who
participated in a program and what they thought about it. Interviews are
especially useful when you need information from those who have
difficulty reading or writing, or when you are considering complex and
sensitive topics or feelings. Although interviews are expensive and take
a great deal of time, they are often invaluable. What better way is there
to give people in the program a chance to speak out?

What Questions Should You Ask, and How?

Don't use evaluation instruments that call for more information than
you need to understand the program. If you want to know how well all
students perform, don't collect data about the differences between girls
and boys. It's particularly important in interviews to focus directly on
what you need, because otherwise, you'll be wasting people's time in
purposeless conversation.

Interviews typically use an interview schedule that lists the questions
to ask, the possible response categories, and leaves room for recording
answers. The interviewer usually records all information on the
interview schedule, but occasionally the respondent may be asked to
complete certain questions.

You can ask questions in several ways. One involves a nominal scale
using categories for a single dimension, such as male or female; single,
married, divorced, separated, or widowed.

Here's an example of a nominal scale:

Example 73   A Nominal Scale

Which of the following best describes your job on the project? (Hand card to interviewee.) Just give me the letter of the best answer. (Place an "X" in the appropriate space.)

_____ A. Project coordinator
_____ B. Evaluator
_____ C. Educational expert
_____ D. Secretary/clerk
_____ E. No answer

An ordinal-scale item records data in the form of ranks rather than in some absolute amount. As in the following example, this scale is usually used to reflect people's feelings or attitudes.

Example 74   An Ordinal Scale

The following questions are about your job on the project and how you feel about it. (Hand card to interviewee.) Considering everything, how satisfied are you? (Circle the appropriate number.)

	Very Satisfied	Satisfied	Neither Satisfied nor Dis-satisfied	Dis-satisfied	Not Very Satisfied
With your job?	5	4	3	2	1
With your pay?	5	4	3	2	1
With your colleagues?	5	4	3	2	1

The interval scale question asks for information that can be categorized in terms of absolute values. For example:

Example 75   An Interval Scale

Which describes your annual family income? (Mark the interviewee's choice.)

_____ Under $10,000
_____ $10,000-$20,000
_____ Over $20,000
_____ Don't know
_____ No answer

Open-ended questions are also used in interviews:

Please give me at least two qualities you look for in a project coordinator.

1. _____
2. _____

Interview questions are sometimes accompanied by probes. Try probes to get a more complete answer than you got the first time, or to clarify a response that is confusing, irrelevant, or suspected of being untrue.

Example 76   Probes

What do you think should be done about the time you have to wait to see a doctor?

Probe:

- What do you personally think should be done?
- Should anything be done?
- What should be done?
- Should anything else be done?

Some answers that need to be probed for more information:

- It's really time to do something about the problem.
- There's been a lot of complaining about it.
- Something should be done.
- The doctors will object.
- I don't have any idea what should be done.

Remember that probes must not suggest responses. To avoid this, use probes like, "Anything else?" Be as tactful as possible when using probes so you won't sound as though you're challenging the respondent. Try to convey the idea that the person's opinions are so important that you want to be sure you understand and include them all.

Here are some tips for organizing your interview forms or schedules:

- Don't clutter the instrument by putting too much on a page. This makes it hard for the interviewer to read, and it may keep the respondent from answering fully, especially with open-ended questions.

- Keep the format consistent. If you use italics for the interviewer, don't use them for the interviewees.
- Have only one question on each line.
- Make sure you include a "no answer" category.
- Whenever necessary, include a "don't know" or "other" category. You may not be able to anticipate everyone's response in advance.
- Pretest the interview schedule with a sample of people from the group who will be interviewed. That's the only way to be sure you will get the information you need in the form you need it, and within a reasonable amount of time. Pretesting is the key to reliable and valid information.

When you pretest the interview, don't forget to try out your methods for recording the results. Interviewers may record answers on the form right away, tape record the interview, or compile notes at the conclusion of the session. Too much writing while someone is talking may seem rude; too little writing may be mistaken for indifference.

Who Should Ask the Questions and Who Might Answer?

Interviewers should "fit in" as well as possible with respondents. They should avoid flamboyant clothes, haircuts, and so on. Sometimes it's a good idea to select interviewers who are like the respondents. If you want to find out why adolescent girls smoke, for example, you might hire young women to do the questioning.

It's also important that interviewers be able to speak clearly and understandably. Those with unusual speech patterns or accents may provoke an unnecessarily favorable or unfavorable reaction. An interviewer who is more attractive and likable than another may get more favorable responses.

Training is essential to ensure that all interviewers know what's expected of them and that they ask all questions in the same fashion within the same amount of time. Always provide practice in conducting interviews. You can have interviewers practice on each other.

It's a good idea to hand out written instructions for people to take with them. These should summarize the essentials of the interview and list telephone numbers and other important information. Try to anticipate some problems and offer solutions. Here's one example:

Example 77   An Interviewing Problem

Problem: You telephone the respondent at the appointed time but no one answers.

Solution: Call every five minutes until the end of the time allotted for the interview (half hour). If you get the person in 15 minutes, complete the interview. If you get the person after that, arrange a new appointment. (Use the attached schedule or fit them into other slots left by cancellations.) If you don't get the person at all, record the information on the sheet called Missing Data Record.

Choose the people to interview because you especially need or want their information. That usually means you must decide whether to include everyone particpating in the evaluation (sometimes not financially possible) or just a sample. Some common strategies are random sampling, random stratified sampling, and purposive sampling.

Random sampling means that everyone has an equal probability of being selected. If you want to conduct 45 interviews but you have 100 people, you could put their names in a hat and select them one by one. Or you could be more scientific and use a table of random numbers found in statistics textbooks.

If you want to make sure that you have a sample of men and women that mirrors your population of 100 people, you might have to use random stratified sampling. If you have 80 men and 20 women (a ratio of 4 to 1), then you would select one woman at random for every four men until you have nine women and 36 men for a total of 45 people.

Sometimes, however, you have some people you feel must be interviewed. That's when you use purposive sampling. Suppose you are evaluating a hospital's orientation program for new nurses. You might decide to interview all new nurses, but only a sample of the other nurses and supervisors.

How Should You Conduct the Interview?

Here are some suggestions for the interviewer:

- Make a brief introductory statement that will
  - —describe who is conducting the interview (John Williams for Reynolds Memorial Medical Center),
  - —tell why it is being conducted (to find out how satisfied you are with our hospitality program),
  - —explain why you are calling the respondent (we're asking a random sample of people who were discharged from the hospital in the last two months),
  - —indicate whether or not answers will be kept confidential (your name will not be used without your written permission).

- Impress the person you're talking to with the importance of the interview and of the answers. People are more likely to cooperate if they value what is being called for. Don't promise to deal with every complaint or criticism, but suggest that all answers will receive equal attention.

- Be flexible. Although it's important to stay on schedule and to ask all the questions, a few people might have trouble hearing you or understanding some of the questions. If that happens, slow down and repeat the question.

- Interview people alone. The presence of another person may be distracting and alter the results.

- Ask questions just as they appear on the interview schedule. It's important to ask everyone the same questions in the same way or the results won't be comparable. Suppose one interviewer asks, "Is program X better than program Y?" and another interviewer asks, "Is program Y better than program X?" Logically the questions may be the same, but the prompts are very different. Be sure, also, to ask every question.

- Follow all instructions given at the training session and described on the interview form. Sometimes instructions involve the sequence of questions, such as, "Ask question 10 only if the answer to question 9 is no," or "Ask question 11 only if the answer to question 9 is yes."

HOW TO USE SIMULATIONS

A *simulation* is an information collection technique that evaluators use when they want to find out how well people perform when they're on the job. Sometimes simulations are called *performance tests* or *tasks*, and require trained individuals to "pretend" to need services from a program's staff. The staff's responses are then analyzed to see if they are adequate. Examples of simulations include having the evaluator ask librarians for information and appraise the information's correctness and the courtesy with which it is given or having the evaluator call a local welfare office and monitor the time it takes to get satisfactory assistance. The major advantage of simulations is that they mimic real-world activities and therefore, result in extremely believable and accurate data. Their major disadvantages are that they are usually time consuming and expensive. In this section, we are going to describe a simulation procedure for evaluating any educational or social service that can be given over the telephone. It is based on one that has been used to evaluate a cancer information effort designed to help the public get the best medical information currently available. The simulation has four steps:

(1) Write scripts for "pretend" callers.
(2) Create evaluation forms.
(3) Select and train the callers.
(4) Make the calls.

Writing Scripts for Callers

The first step in the simulation process is to decide on the types of people who are likely to use the service being evaluated and the problems they have so that simulations can be prepared. For the cancer service evaluation, the simulations take the form of two scenarios of the needs of "typical" patients. In the first, the caller is a young woman whose husband is severely disabled because of cancer and has begun to drink. The second caller is frightened of breast cancer. Here are the scenarios for the two callers.

Example 78   Simulated Calls

Simulated Call 1: Psychosocial

Summary/Background:

Caller is a 24-year-old married woman with two children, ages 3 and 4, whose husband, 26 years old, had his right leg removed because of bone cancer. He does not want an artificial leg, has changed completely, and has begun to drink, making life hard for her and the kids. Husband is an unemployed former construction worker and stays home with the kids. She works as a hairdresser and her address is 1233 La Brea Ave., Los Angeles, CA 90099. They live off her income and his disability payments. They have an oncologist, and they're not currently seeing any doctor.

Script:

"My name is Frances Latimer. I don't know if this is the kind of problem you people deal with, but I'm calling because of my husband. Two years ago he had his leg removed because of cancer and he hasn't been the same since. I mean, he really used to be a really easy-going person and now he's just horrible to live with and he's been drinking all the time now. He loses his temper with me and with the kids all the time now, too. I don't know what to do anymore. One of my friends at work suggested I call you."

(If volunteer tries to counsel caller, caller is to say she is calling from work and has to get off the phone.)

Simulated Call 2: Information

Summary/Background:

Caller is a 32-year-old married woman with no children who has recently discovered a lump in her left breast. There is no family history of breast cancer. She doesn't know if she has cystic disease and doesn't check her breasts regularly. She has seen her GP but has not told her husband about this yet.

Script:

"I wonder if you could help me. I'm sort of confused. The other day I found a lump in my left breast and called my doctor. He's a GP and so he referred me to a doctor in his building who is a surgeon. This surgeon says he wants to do a biopsy as soon as possible to find out if it is cancer.

He says if it is cancer, he wants to remove my breast. Is that the right thing to do? I mean . . . what if he makes a mistake? I don't know . . . I mean, what should I do?

One of my friends suggested I call you."
(If volunteer tries to counsel caller, caller is to say she is calling from work and has to get off the phone.)

Creating Evaluation Forms

It is absolutely essential that the evaluator know just what the simulated phone call is to accomplish so that the appropriate evaluation instruments can be prepared. For example, the cancer service is staffed by trained volunteers, and the funding agency wants to know if they provide callers with accurate information. Also, the agency is concerned that the volunteers be clear and emphatic. The evaluators have decided that the trained callers—none of whom is a cancer expert—would not be able to assess accuracy, but they could give their opinions of clarity and empathy. Thus a form was developed that callers complete at the end of each encounter with the cancer information staff. To minimize paper work, the instrument requires very little writing (Example 79).

To get accuracy, the evaluators decided to analyze the Call Completion Record, which volunteers regularly fill out upon finishing each call. A properly completed Call Completion Form for the woman whose husband feared an artificial leg is shown in Example 80. The evaluators would check the accuracy of the Call Completion Record by using the checklist presented in Example 81.

Selecting and Training Callers

Callers must be extensively trained to make the calls, fill out the forms, and follow the schedule of calls. The training package should contain, at the minimum, a description of the evaluation's purposes, complete step-by-step instructions for making the calls, and explanations of the each of the terms used in the form completed by the pretend callers. Here's part of the training package for the cancer information evaluation:

Instructions for Callers

Use of Script

(1) *Locating the appropriate volunteer.* The caller is to make a simulated telephone call, using the appropriate scripts, to each volunteer according to schedule for that month. According to the monthly schedule, more than one volunteer may be scheduled at

(text continues on p. 167)

Example 79   Evaluation Forms

Evaluation Form: Call 1

Name of Caller _____   Volunteer_____

Date of Call _____   Call length _____ min.

Time call began _____

Time call ended _____

Essential:	Yes	No
1. Makes referral to XYZ Psychosocial Counseling Line 1-800-XXX-XXXX	_____	_____

Acceptable:	Yes	No
1. Makes referral to other mental health facility	_____	_____

_____

_____

Unacceptable:	Yes	No
1. Volunteer tried to counsel caller; call terminated	_____	_____

Caller Perception of Volunteer:

	4	3	2	1
Empathy	Very Satisfactory	Satisfactory	Unsatisfactory	Very Unsatisfactory

	4	3	2	1
Clarity	Very Good	Good	Poor	Very Poor

Other Comments/Quotes:

Example 80 A Completed Form

OPERATOR **PAM**	CALL BEGINS **2 pm**	DATE **10-24-80**
RESEARCH OFF PHONE	CALL ENDS **2:10 pm**	☐ MAIL ☐ WALK-IN
LENGTH CALL BACK	CALL LENGTH **10 min**	NON-ENGLISH LANG.

CALLER'S NAME **Francis Latimer** AGE ___ ☐ MALE ☐ FEMALE

ADDRESS **1233 La Brea Ave.** PHONE ( )

CITY **L.A.** STATE **CA** ZIP **90099**

WHERE CALLER LEARNED OF SERVICE:

ACS	HEALTH PROF.	MAGAZINE _____
BROCHURE	NEWSPAPER	RADIO _____
CCC/LA	PHONE BOOK	T.V. _____
X FRIEND	REPEAT CALLER	OTHER _____

SITE

1. BLADDER	14. LEUKEMIA	27. RECTUM
2. X BONE	15. LIP	28. SALIVARY GLAND
3. BRAIN	16. LIVER	29. SKIN
4. BREAST	17. LUNG	30. STOMACH
5. BRONCHUS	18. LYMPHOMA	31. TESTIS
6. CERVIX	19. MELANOMA	32. THYROID
7. COLON	20. MULTI. MYE-	33. TONGUE
8. ESOPHAGUS	LOMA	34. TRACHEA
9. EYE	21. MOUTH	35. UTERUS
10. HEART	22. NOSE	36. VAGINA
11. HODGKIN'S	23. OVARY	37. VULVA
12. KIDNEY	24. PANCREAS	38. OTHER
13. LARYNX	25. PENIS	39. CHILDRENS CA
	26. PROSTATE	40. METASTATIC CA

INQUIRY ____   PATIENT'S AGE ____

TYPE OF CALLER

GENERAL PUBLIC	MEDIA
CANCER PATIENT	HEALTH PROF.
X FAMILY/FRIEND	
	(TYPE)

WHY CALLER IS USING SERVICE

CONCERN/HAVING CANCER	X REFERRAL/SER-
CONCERN/MEDIA STORY	VICE REQUEST
CASE SPECIFIC INFO.	GENERAL INFO.
CONFIRM PHYS. INFO.	
X EMOTIONAL SUPPORT	(OTHER)

IS THE PATIENT SEEING AN ONCOLOGIST? ☐ YES ☒ NO

DOES THE PATIENT HAVE A DR.? ☒ YES ☐ NO

INQUIRY TYPES

1	AGENCY/SERV. INFO.		HOSPICE
	ACS		HOSPITAL/CLIN.
	SCREENING CENTERS		ONCOLOGIST
	REHABILITATION		OTHER _____
2	SITE INFO.	13	RELATED MED.
3	CIS/USC		COND.
4	DIET/NUTRITION	14	
5	DONATION		RISK FACTOR
6	ED. PROG. MATERIALS		(TYPE)
7	FINANCIAL AID	15	CHEMOTHERAPY
8	GEN. CANCER INFO.	16	IMMUNOTHERAPY
9		17	RADIATION THER.
	DIAGNOSTIC PROCED.	18	SURGERY
10	NON-CANCER	19	☐
11	PATIENT RIGHTS		UNPROVEN METH-
12	X REFERRAL		OD (TYPE)
	ACS		☐ LAETRILE
	BET CENTER	20	OTHER _____
	X COUNSELING		☐ EXPERIMENTAL
			TREATMENT
			☐ RESEARCH
			☐ STATISTICS
			☐ SMOKING CESSA-
			TION

INQUIRY

Husband has had leg amputated. Doesn't want artificial leg. Has begun to drink and take it out on family.

RESPONSE

Recommend XYZ counseling line

DISCLAIMER (LAY CALLS ONLY) ☒ USED

PLEASE DISCUSS THE INFORMATION I HAVE GIVEN YOU WITH A PHYSICIAN. I AM NOT A DOCTOR. ONLY A PHYSICIAN, WITH THE AID OF A COMPLETE MEDICAL HISTORY AND A PHYSICAL EXAM, CAN GIVE ADVICE IN A PARTICULAR CASE.

Example 81   Call Record Form Evaluation
Checklist: Call #1

	Correct	Incorrect	Missing
Operator (fill in name)	____	____	____
Call begins (fill in time)	____	____	____
Call ends (fill in time)	____	____	____
Call length (fill in duration)	____	____	____
Date (fill in date)	____	____	____
Caller's name (fill in)	____	____	____
Caller's address (fill in)	____	____	____
Sex (female)	____	____	____
Zip (fill in)	____	____	____
where caller learned of CIS (friend)	____	____	____
Type of caller (family/friend)	____	____	____
Why caller is using service (emotional support, refer- ral/service request)	____	____	____
Is patient seeing an on- cologist? (no)	____	____	____
Does the patient have a doctor? (yes)	____	____	____
Inquiry types (referral, counseling)	____	____	____
Site (bone)	____	____	____

Inquiry: Woman's husband refuses artificial leg: Has begun to drink and give children a bad time	____	____	____
Response: Recommend: Call XYZ Counseling line	____	____	____
Disclaimer	____	____	____

any given time. In order to ensure that the caller does not reach a given counselor more than once, it may be necessary to ask for a volunteer by his or her first name. The most natural way to do this, without raising the suspicion of the person answering the phone is for the caller to say, "A friend of mine suggested I call here. May I please speak to _____ ?"

(2) *Using the script.* Using a different fabricated name each time, callers are requested to stick to the script as closely as possible. Additional information for which the volunteer might ask is included in the short summary above the script. The caller is requested to refrain from volunteering any other information. Extraneous or highly personal questions concerning religion, education, income, and so forth should be fielded by the caller. However, the caller might jot down at the end of the Caller Evaluation Form under Comments that such questions were asked. When in doubt about the answer to a volunteer's question the caller should say "I don't know," "I don't feel like talking about that," "I've got to get off the phone soon," and so on.

(3) *Completing the caller evaluation form.*

- The caller should write in his or her name, the time the call is started, the time the call ends, the length of time (in minutes) that it takes to complete the call, and the volunteer who fielded the call.

- The caller should indicate whether or not the disclaimer was used, and, if appropriate, whether the information/referral disclaimer was used (check off yes or no).

- The caller should show whether or not the volunteer offered to send written material. Check off yes or no. However, this is optional since for calls 1 and 2, the caller declines to give address or phone number.

- On the empathy and clarity scale, circle the number that best represents the degree of empathy and clarity demonstrated by the volunteer. Definitions and explanations of empathy and clarity are attached.

- Under Comments/Quotes, the caller should note any inappropriate questions or suggestions made by the volunteer, as well as any incorrect information.

- Call #1: *Under "Essential" (best answer):* Volunteer should refer caller to UCLA Psychosocial Counseling Line (1-800-XXX-7422). Caller should note carefully whether volunteer gave correct number. Check off yes or no.

- *Under "Acceptable":* Volunteer identifies caller's need for counseling and refers caller to another service. Caller should write down referral and check off yes or no.

- *Under "Unacceptable":* Volunteer did not identify call as psychosocial and/or tried to counsel caller. Check off yes or no.

- *Clarity (of communication):* Clarity refers to the quality of the response that the counselor gives to the caller. The counselor must answer simply and clearly the requests of the caller for information. There should be no doubt in the mind of the caller, no matter how distraught he or she is, of what information the counselor conveyed. Not only should the answers be technically correct, but they should be comprehended by the caller no matter what his or her educational level, knowledge of the subject matter, or state of mind. Somewhat more objective and therefore easier to measure, clarity of communication or response would be reflected by agreement with the following statements when describing the counselor (volunteer):

  — He (or she) understands what I tell him (her).

  — He (or she) responds to my questions and inquiries.

  — I understand what he (or she) told me.

  — I feel satisfied enough with the information I received that I do not have to call the counselor back or call another counselor to have my questions answered.

— He (or she) allows me to have enough time to write down the information (refers to names, addresses, and telephone numbers).

For the purpose of this study the clarity (of communication) scale is a 4-point scale, ranging from 4 (very good) to 1 (very poor), also located toward the end of the Caller Evaluation Form.

Making the Calls

Here are some concerns that must be addressed to make the simulations effective:

- Should the program staff be told about the simulations? Yes. The staff should be aware that an evaluation is in process and that at some time, a pretend call will be made. Staff should be encouraged to participate, but should probably be given the option to withdraw.

- Make sure that each staff person is contacted at least twice. After all, everyone is entitled to one bad day. If a particular staff person appears to have been really good one time and rather poor the next, a third simulation might be necessary.

- Make sure that you have allocated enough time to contact all staff members. Remember that some people might be part of the simulation numerous times. In the cancer information evaluation, there are 30 staff members being called with 3 scenarios or, 90 calls. To avoid anyone's catching on to when the calls are being made, a three-month period is being set aside for the simulations.

- Make sure that each caller is likely to get the same information as the others from all simulations. Good training and frequent retraining enhances interrater reliability.

HOW TO EVALUATE ATTITUDES

Evaluators are frequently asked to find out how participants feel about a program. Are people satisfied? Has the staff's morale improved? Which of the three programs did people like best? Did the participants think the program was worth the money? Although we may

Example 82 Attitudinal Evaluation Questions

Directions: The statements below are opinions. They reflect unresolved issues, and there are no right or wrong answers. Please indicate how you feel about the statements by checking how strongly you agree or disagree with each.

	Strongly Agree	Agree	Neutral	Disagree	Strongly Disagree
1. Evaluating attitudes is important.	___			___	___
2. Knowing how people behave is more important than knowing how they feel.	___	___	___	___	___
3. Evaluating attitudes is too complicated.	___	___	___	___	___
4. Evaluators have no business dealing with attitudes.	___	___	___	___	___
5. Evaluating attitudes is a challenge.	___	___	___	___	___

disagree over how much emphasis to place on evaluating attitudes, most people believe it's important to learn what participants in a program think about it. Evaluation questions that ask about feelings, interests, beliefs, and values are called *attitudinal* questions (see Example 82).

Current knowledge of human development suggests that there is an intricate relationship between how people feel about things, what they know, and how they behave. Knowing the facts about good nutrition may not persuade young people to eat balanced meals, for example, but if they believe their appearance is important in making friends, they may be more likely to stick to a wholesome diet.

Evaluating how people feel is extremely complicated. Definitions of emotions are complex, and it takes a great deal of time and money to develop reliable and valid measures. What is love, fear, hate, anger? How can you tell a "normally" angry person from one who is not normal?

To complicate matters further, some people believe that evaluators have no business questioning people's private attitudes or feelings, except perhaps on a very elementary level. It's okay to ask patients if they're satisfied with their care at XYZ hospital, but is it ethical to ask them how they feel about Dr. Smith? We believe evaluating attitudes is important, complicated and difficult. Like most evaluators, we've found it's a real challenge. One of the most common ways to find out about attitudes, is to ask people to tell you about themselves. In measurement language, this is called a *self-report*.

The Likert Scale

Likert scales rely on response categories like strongly agree, agree, undecided, disagree, and strongly disagree. For scoring purposes, strongly agree is usually assigned the maximum weight say, of 5 points, while strongly disagree is given the minimum weight say, of 1 point. Example 83 shows an item that uses a Likert-type scale.

Likert scales are relatively easy to use, score, and interpret. But you will have to contend with the *halo effect* occasionally. A patient may rate hospital care as excellent on the day of discharge, for example, and still come up with negative ratings on the day the bills come in. You will also find that a few people always seem to select the neutral or middle category, no matter what.

Example 83   Likert Scale

Directions: Should the government assume the cost of the following?
Check the box that best describes your feelings.

	Strongly Disapprove (1)	Disapprove (2)	Undecided (3)	Approve (4)	Strongly Approve (5)
Health Insurance	☐	☐	☐	☐	☐
Abortion	☐	☐	☐	☐	☐
Renal Dialysis	☐	☐	☐	☐	☐
Homemaker Services	☐	☐	☐	☐	☐
Medical Care for Veterans	☐	☐	☐	☐	☐

Be sure that your items truly distinguish people with "good" attitudes from those with "bad" attitudes. In other words, people who like the program should score higher than people who don't. Pilot test and validate your scale to make sure of this before you use it.

The Semantic Differential

Here you ask people to indicate their feelings about a particular topic by checking some point on a scale between opposites, such as good and bad. For example:

PSYCHOTHERAPY

Fast ____ : ____ : ____ : ____ : ____ : ____ Slow

Good ____ : ____ : ____ : ____ : ____ : ____ Bad

Worthwhile ____ : ____ : ____ : ____ : ____ : ____ Valuable

Strong ____ : ____ : ____ : ____ : ____ : ____ Weak

Unpleasant ____ : ____ : ____ : ____ : ____ : ____ Pleasant

When properly used, the semantic differential will provide information that sorts out negative attitudes from positive ones. People who prefer psychotherapy will generally view it as fast, good, valuable, strong, and pleasant, while those who don't will generally choose the opposite adjectives.

The creators of the semantic differential technique have grouped adjective pairs into three major categories: evaluation, which includes "good-bad" and "fair-unfair"; potency, which includes "strong-weak" and "heavy-light"; and activity, which includes "fast-slow" and "active-passive." Numerous studies show that you can use the evaluative dimension of the semantic differential to discover people's predominant feelings about a variety of ideas and subjects. Here are some scales you can try:

high-low	kind-cruel
empty-full	healthy-sick
honest-dishonest	rough-smooth
clean-dirty	fair-unfair
relaxed-tense	rich-poor

Forced Choices

Here you confront people with an actual choice between different things, instead of asking them how much they like or disklike something. The number of choices usually ranges from two to four.

I prefer:

_____ 1. a very short waiting time for the doctor.

_____ 2. a doctor who fits people in.

I prefer:

_____ 1. a nurse practitioner to perform the physical examination.

_____ 2. a doctor with all the latest equipment to perform the physical examination.

For these items to be valid, you would have to show that certain groups of respondents will choose them in some systematic way. If you're interested in developing a neighborhood free clinic, you might use these items to find out how many people prefer a private practitioner model (short waiting time and technical equipment) and how many would be happier with a clinic model (nurse practitioner and fitting in patients).

Items using forced choices are relatively difficult to develop because it takes a good sense of what is theoretically possible. Yet they may be more objective than the Likert scale, where people often sense whether agreement or disagreement is preferred. Forced choices are easy to score and interpret.

Observations

Observing people to find out their attitudes has a long history. Most of us have accepted the notion that "seeing is believing," particularly if we all focus on the same factors and make several observations using different raters. Unfortunately, observations are expensive and time consuming because people must be trained to focus their attention on the same things in the same way.

Observations make use of at least three types of rating scales:

Example 84   Rating Scales

Numerical Scales

How often does the teacher assign homework?
_____ 1. Always
_____ 2. Usually
_____ 3. Sometimes
_____ 4. Never

Graphic Scales

Please mark your overall rating of how skillfully the candidate applied CPR (cardiac pulmonary resuscitation).

Very
Skillfully _____ Not Very
Skillfully

     1   2   3   4   5

Checklists

Check whether or not the participant performed each of the following activities.

	Yes	No
Interrupted the discussion	_____	_____
Left the room	_____	_____
Introduced the topic	_____	_____
Clarified a point	_____	_____
Asked for a break	_____	_____
Asked for clarification of an idea	_____	_____

How to Get Around Developing Your Own Measures

Are instruments available? Yes, although limited in number and sometimes in quality, standardized measures are available to you to use in evaluating attitudes. Here are some places to check for good measures:

- Oscar Buros, ed., *Personality Tests and Reviews*, Highland Park, NJ: Gryphon Press, 1970.

- Oscar Buros, ed., *The Seventh Mental Measurements Yearbook*, Highland Park, NJ: Gryphon Press, 1972.

- Comrey, Andrew L., Backer, Thomas E., and Glaser, Edward M., *A Sourcebook for Mental Health Measures*, Los Angeles: Human Interaction Research Institute, 1973.

- Journals such as *Evaluation Review* (Beverly Hills, Sage Publications); *Health and Medical Care Services Review* (New York: Haworth Press).

- Agencies that conduct evaluation studies, such as schools of education, public health, and sociology.

- Clearinghouses for studies in education like Education Research Information Clearinghouse.

- The National Library of Medicine's computerized reference service MEDLINE.

- State and federal agencies that sponsor health services research and evaluation.

- Publishers of psychological tests.

- Chun, K-T., Cobb, S., and French, J.R.P., Jr., *Measures for Psychological Assessment*. Ann Arbor, MI: Institute for Social Science Research, 1978.

Try Surrogate Techniques

Surrogate techniques may enable you to collect information about attitudes by relying on what people do instead of what they say. Here are some you might consider:

- *Money.* The amount of money individuals are willing to spend on certain activities and services can be a reflection of their attitudes.

- *Time.* Time, like money, is a scarce commodity.

- *Fund of information.* The amount or type of information an individual has about objects, people, activities, or issues may reflect his or her interests.

- *Measures of attention or distraction.* Records of the length of time an individual attends to a task may indicate a degree of commitment.

- *Written records or personal documents.* Analysis of diaries, letters, or records may reveal a person's attitudes.

- *Sociometric measures.* Analysis of choice of friends may reveal people's preferences and values.

- *Activity levels.* How excited people become about certain activities and whether they see them through to the end may reflect their choice and interests.

CHAPTER VI

Analyzing Information

ALL EVALUATIONS ACCUMULATE DATA that need to be analyzed. The difference between an efficient evaluation and an inefficient one is that the former collects and analyzes just what is needed to answer the evaluation questions, while the latter may not collect enough relevant data but instead, gathers information that is not really targeted to the program. One way of ensuring efficiency is to focus on the evaluation question. Does it call for descriptions of participant characteristics? (Then make sure you collected information on sex, age, income, and so on, and think of descriptive statistics such as frequency counts and averages.) Does it ask for comparisons among groups on some continuous dimension like a test of knowledge? (Make sure you have a valid test, and think of techniques like ANOVA.)

The first section of this chapter is devoted to helping you choose among analytical techniques to give you answers to some commonly asked evaluation questions. The techniques include descriptive statistics, correlations, and regression analysis. Some tips on analyzing and interpreting data are also given. The second section discusses analysis of variance (ANOVA), a staple in the analytic diet. The next three sections explain three nonparametric techniques, the Mann Whitney U, the chi-square, and the sign test.

HOW TO CHOOSE AND
USE DATA ANALYSIS TECHNIQUES

Data analysis is one of the most important tasks an evaluator has to perform. Even if you don't have to do it yourself, you should understand enough about the basic principles to know what the statistician is doing. The evaluation questions shape the entire evaluation, and you should choose analysis methods that will permit you to answer the questions directly.

Will Descriptive Statistics Answer the Question?

Descriptive statistics describe data in terms of measures of central tendency (mode, median, mean), variability (standard deviation and range), and frequency, such as the number of people getting a total score of 62, 75, 100. They can be used to answer evaluation questions such as:

- Did the number of students performing at grade level increase?
- Did a majority of the participants say the program met their needs?
- How similar were attitudes about national health insurance at the end of the program?

Descriptive statistics are among the most useful analysis techniques for evaluations because they are inherently meaningful and easily understood. They are the units for more complex statistical procedures.

Here's one way descriptive statistics can be used to analyze evaluation information:

Example 85 Simple Descriptive Statistics

Program description: The goal of the program is to teach social workers to improve their interpersonal communication skills. To accomplish this goal, students view videotaped conversations between two persons and are trained to distinguish between what speakers say and what they mean by observing content, tone, context, and body language. The program is judged to be successful if students learn to adequately use content, tone, context, and body language to interpret conversations.

Evaluation question: Are students able to use content, tone, context, and body language to interpret conversations?

Design: A case design was used in which all students who enrolled in selected communication courses participated in the interpersonal communication skills program during three weeks of the fall semester.

The dependent variable was an ability to interpret conversations as measured by an achievement test. The independent variable was studied at only one level: participation in the interpersonal communication skills program.

Information collection plan: A test was given to all participating students at the end of the course. The highest possible score on the test was 100 points, with adequate performance defined as a score of 70 or better.

Analysis plan: Descriptive statistics were computed from students' total test scores at the end of the three-week program.

Analysis results:

$\overline{X}$	SD	N	Range	Number of Students Who Achieved a Score of 70 or Better
78.8	13.6	130	44 – 96	71

Interpretation: A total of 130 students (N = 130) completed the program. Their average score ($\overline{X}$) was 78.8 points, which is above the criterion, and 71 students demonstrated an adequate ability to interpret conversation. The relatively small standard deviation (SD) and range indicate that each student's ability is similar to the others.

Should You Use Correlation Statistics?

Correlations measure the relationship between two variables, a dependent variable and an independent variable—for example, number of years of schooling and salary. They are reported within a range of +1 (perfect positive correlation) to –1 (perfect negative correlation).

When high values on one variable occur simultaneously with high values on another, the two variables are said to be positively correlated, and when high values on one variable occur with low values on another, the two variables are said to be negatively correlated.

Correlations can be used to answer evaluation questions such as:

- What is the relationship between self-concept and the number of visits to the school nurse?

- Can scores on college entrance examinations be used to identify people who are likely to succeed in the new management training program?
- Is vocational preference correlated with parents' jobs?

Warning: You can use correlations to identify relationships between variables, but you cannot use them to establish causation. A correlation analysis can show that people who have completed many years of schooling usually earn high salaries, but it cannot show that people earn high salaries *because* they had many years of schooling.

Here's one way correlation statistics might be used to analyze evaluation information:

Example 86   Correlation Statistics

Program description: The goal of the program is to improve fourth grade students' reading ability. Teachers for the program have been selected because they have at least three years of teaching experience and have master's degrees in reading education. The program takes place throughout the school year and occupies one hour a day of each student's time. The program is considered successful if, at the end of the year, students' reading levels are above the national norm.

Evaluation background: Preliminary evaluation findings indicated that some students did very well with the program, while others did badly, and the evaluator was asked to identify factors that distinguished among them. One of the factors studied was birth order.

Evaluation question: Is there a relationship between birth order and success in the program? (Birth order refers to whether a child is the first born, second born, and so on.)

Design: A case design was used for the evaluation, and it included all students who participated in the program. The dependent variable was success in the program, as measured by students' scores on an achievement test. The independent variable was students' birth order.

Information collection plan: A 500-point, nationally normed achievement test was given to all participating fourth grade students at the end of the school year. Students' birth orders were determined from school records.

Analysis plan: Students' raw scores on the reading-achievement test and their birth orders were correlated, using the Pearson Product Moment Formula.

Analysis results: A correlation coefficient (r) of –0.89 was obtained based on data from 206 students.

N = 206
r = –.89
r^2 = .79

Interpretation: A high negative correlation (r = –.89) was found between students' reading scores and their birth orders, indicating that 79% (r^2 = .79) of the total variation in students' reading scores could be accounted for by their position of birth. This finding suggests that first- and second-born students are more successful with the program (have higher reading scores) than the others. (It cannot be concluded that first- and second born students are necessarily smarter.)

Is Regression Analysis the Technique You Need?

Regression is a method for examining the relationship between a dependent variable and two or more independent variables. If there is only one independent variable, then regression is the same as correlation statistics.

Regression can be used to predict the value of a dependent variable based on values of one or more independent variables. Regression analysis can also be used to answer this question:

What is the relationship between students' mathematics performance (the dependent variable) and the number of hours of instruction received, grade level, and sex (the three independent variables)?

You can express the answer to that question mathematically as an equation of the following form:

y =	w_1x_1	+	w_2x_2	+	w_3x_3	+	c
Dependent Variable	weight 1		weight 2		weight 3		Constant
	Independent Variable 1		Independent Variable 2		Independent Variable 3		
(Students' Mathematics Performance)	(Number of Hours of Instruction Received)		(Grade Level)		(Sex)		

This equation shows the relationship between a dependent variable (y) and three independent variables (x_1, x_2, x_3). The weights (w_1, w_2, w_3) or regression coefficients are computed as part of the analysis and reflect the contribution of each independent variable in explaining the dependent variable.

That is, if w_1 is greater than w_2 and w_3, then x_1 is the independent variable that contributes most to an understanding of y, the dependent variable. (For such interpretations to be made, x_1, x_2, and x_3 must be measured using the same metric, or alternately, w_1, w_2, and w_3 must be normalized or standardized as part of the computations for the regression analysis.)

Here's an example of how you might use regression analysis if you were evaluating a high school program for disruptive students:

Example 87   Regression

Program description: The purpose of the program is to teach stress management and self-discipline skills to high school students with behavior problems so that they can be placed in a regular classroom. Specifically trained teachers instruct students and their parents in how to recognize the early warning signs of behavioral outbursts, how to treat them, and when to seek assistance. Teachers and students together decide how many hours students should be counseled. Fewer classroom disruptions are considered evidence of the program's merit.

Evaluation background: Preliminary evaluation data showed that some students received only 5 hours of counseling, while others received as many as 25 hours. The average was 10 hours per student. Since counselor salaries represent the major cost of the program, you have been asked to investigate the relationship between the number of classroom disruptions and the number of hours students are counseled, taking into account their age and the severity of their behavior problems.

Evaluation question: What is the relationship between number of classroom disruptions and (1) hours of counseling, (2) severity of behavior problems at the beginning of the program, and (3) age?

Design: You chose a case design for the evaluation. The dependent variable was the number of times a student caused a classroom disruption during the months of December through May. The independent variables were (1) the number of hours of counseling a student received, (2) the severity of the student's behavior problem at the beginning of the program and (3) the student's age. The evaluation included all high school students who were identified by the district as having behavior problems severe enough to warrant being taken from the regular classroom and placed in a special one.

Information collection plan: You reviewed school records to obtain information about a student's age. You gave teachers special forms to document the nature and frequency of classroom disruptions. You asked counselors to rate the severity of their students' behavior problems at the beginning of the program using a 9-point scale, with 1 as "extremely mild" and 9 as "extremely severe." You also asked them to keep records of how many hours they spent counseling each student throughout the program.

Analysis plan: You conducted a multiple-regression analysis, transforming the weights for each independent variable so that you could report them in terms of the same 10-point scale used in the regression equation.

$$y \quad = \quad 5.01x_1 \quad - \quad 2.11x_2 \quad + \quad 0.07x_3 \quad + \quad 25.01$$

Number of Disruptions	Severity of Behavior Problem	Hours in Counseling	Age

$R^2 = .85$

Interpretation: The results of a multiple-regression analysis demonstrated a relationship between number of classroom disruptions and severity of a students' behavior problem, number of hours of counseling received, and age. In particular, the more severe the problem, the greater the number of disruptions. With more hours of counseling, however, fewer disruptions can be expected. Furthermore, a student's age does not affect this pattern.

These findings suggest that if a student received more counseling, the number of disruptions could be reduced. For example, by increasing counseling hours from ten to fifteen, the expected number of disruptions could be decreased from 14.97 to 4.43 for a 15-year-old student with a severity rating of 2, and from 45.03 to 34.49 for a 15-year-old with a severity rating of 8, a reduction of 10.54 disruptions in both cases.

Analyzing Evaluation Information: Some Tips

Analyzing evaluation information includes:

- pilot testing the information analysis,
- conducting the analysis,
- interpreting the results of the analysis, and
- making recommendations if requested.

Pilot Testing

Information analysis techniques must be pilot tested to find out if they work. If the techniques don't work properly, they must be redesigned. A pilot test should include all the planned information analysis activities and should reveal whether:

- needed information will be available in manageable form,
- necessary expert personnel and special equipment such as computers are available, and
- data reduction procedures are efficient and accurate.

Conducting the Analysis

Once the information analysis techniques have been pilot tested and revised, the evaluator can collect and begin to analyze the information. Sometimes evaluation questions require more than one analysis; other times further analysis is unnecessary unless warranted by the results. For example, to answer the evaluation question, "Which of four programs is most effective in teaching subject X?" you could use a statistical method such as one-way analysis of variance. You would test the hypothesis that there is no difference in average program effectiveness. If the results confirm the hypothesis, then no further analysis would be called for. If, however, the results disprove the hypothesis, you would need additional analysis to find out which programs are responsible for the differences.

An ordered approach to information analysis is the most efficient, yet evaluators often have the notion that most is best. Be careful—security gained from doing all manner of analyses is often illusory. A desultory approach to information analysis is technically unsound because

- it increases the probability of finding significant results by chance alone;

- it results in a loss of credibility as the evaluator strays from the plan specifically tailored to answer the evaluation question; and

- it is hopelessly inefficient.

Interpreting Results

Assume that data collection and analysis have gone smoothly. What does the evaluator do with the results?

As an example: An evaluation question asked whether consumers asked for generic rather than brand-name drugs. A survey questionnaire showed that 40% of the respondents said they did ask for drugs by generic names. The evaluator now has to consider the following three questions:

(1) Is 40% sufficient to prove the program's effectiveness?
(2) Were the respondents representative of all consumers?
(3) Does a positive response (saying they asked for generics) mean the respondents actually chose the generics over the brand-name drugs?

These questions are typical of problems underlying many evaluations. The first deals with standards of program merit, the second with design strategy and sampling procedures, and the third with validity of information collection and analysis methods. (The last question also points out the importance of asking the right evaluation question in the first place. Was the evaluation trying to find out whether the consumers asked for generics, or whether they actually bought generics?) If the evaluation is well organized and carefully thought out, then the information gathered can be interpreted with a minimum of trouble.

Once you have interpreted the analysis results for each evaluation question, you can look at the analyses collectively to get an idea of the effectiveness of the program as a whole. Such overall interpretation is useful in getting a feel for program dynamics or for the relationship among parts of the program.

Interpreting results also involves distinguishing beween statistical and programmatic significance. Statistical significance tells you whether an outcome makes a difference in terms of program goals—that is, whether the outcome justifies the time, effort, and money spent.

Statistical significance and programmatic significance are analogous to reliability and validity. Like reliability, statistical significance is a measure of precision; like validity, programmatic significance is a measure of efficacy and cogency.

Making Recommendations

Finally, analytical results point to obvious recommendations as to how to improve or certify the effectiveness of a program. The evaluator, however, is not always expected to make—and the client is never obligated to accept—such recommendations.

For the generic drug information evaluation, the evaluator supplied the following recommendations when asked:

Example 88   Generic Drug Information Evaluation

Our analysis using descriptive statistics reveals that consumers between 20 and 40 years old meet the standards set for asking for generic drugs, while shoppers between 40 and 60 years old do not. We therefore recommend that you continue to encourage pharmacists to ask older people whether they are willing to use generic drug substitutes.

HOW TO USE ANOVA

Analysis of variance, or ANOVA, is one of the most useful statistical procedures available for analyzing evaluation data. If you want to compare different groups or study changes that take place in the same group from one time to the next, the analysis of variance is a method you should consider. Here's how to proceed:

Take a Careful Look at the Evaluation Question to Be Sure ANOVA Is Appropriate

Remember, ANOVA is used to make comparisons among groups or across times. Here are examples of questions that could be answered using one-way analysis of variance:

(1) Do patients in the experimental program have different compliance rates than patients in the traditional program?
(2) Do experimental patients change their compliance pattern from the beginning to the end of the year?

Decide Which Comparisons to Make and State Your Hypotheses

Once the evaluation questions are posed, you are ready to decide which comparisons you want to make. For example, in Evaluation Question 1 ("Do patients in the experimental program have different compliance rates than patients in the traditional program"), you will compare persons in the experimental and the traditional programs in terms of their compliance.

To evaluate comparisons you must restate the question as a proposition or hypothesis to be accepted or rejected. You could rephrase Evaluation Question 1 in two ways.

- Hypothesis 1: On the average, patients in the experimental program and patients in the traditional program have different compliance rates.

- Hypothesis 2: On the average, patients in the experimental program and patients in the traditional program have the same compliance rate.

Because of its mathematical structure, ANOVA cannot prove directly that there are differences among groups. It can only prove that they aren't the same. To use ANOVA properly, you must test hypotheses about the sameness or equality of behavior and not the differences. For Evaluation Question 1, for instance, you would have to use Hypothesis 2. Ths is called the *null hypothesis:*

Null Hypothesis for Evaluation Question 2: The experimental patients' compliance pattern is the same at the beginning and end of the year.

Make Sure You Have the Data You Need in the Form You Need

ANOVA depends on the use of arithmetic averages and standard deviations. You can't use ANOVA to test a hypothesis about the equality of two groups' behavior unless you have a way to determine their mean performance. Behavior can be measured using tests, observations, ratings, questionnaires, interviews, chart audits, or other program documents.

Test the Hypotheses and Report the Results

Hypotheses are tested with an F statistic, which is derived mathematically using the ANOVA formulas. In general, if the F statistic resulting from the ANOVA is a small number, then the hypothesis cannot be rejected. For Question 1, a small F value would mean that you could not disprove the hypothesis that experimental and traditional patients' compliance rates are the same.

To test hypotheses, first compute means and standard deviations. Apply the ANOVA procedure to these descriptive statistics to get an F statistic. You will find formulas for analysis of variance in standard statistics texts, but canned computer programs are usually available and should probably be used. ANOVA is not a procedure that readily lends itself to hand calculations.

Statistical tables are available that list the smallest value that an F statistic can take in order to reject a hypothesis. These tables provide F values for different degrees of freedom (df) and significance levels (p). Degrees of freedom are the number of independent scores (or observations) entering into the computation of the statistic. The level of significance (p) refers to the probability of falsely rejecting the hypothesis. Evaluators usually use the .05 or .01 significance level, which means that there are either five chances in 100 or one chance in 100 that the hypothesis will be rejected unintentionally.

The results of a one-way ANOVA frequently are displayed in the following way:

One-Way ANOVA

Source of Variation	Degrees of Freedom (df)	F Value	Level of Significance (p)

The sources of variation column names the hypothesis being tested (e.g., male and female patients' compliance rates are the same) and the error term for the analysis (a mathematical result).

The following is a typical report of the use of a one-way ANOVA to answer one evaluation question for an experimental program.

Example 89   One-Way ANOVA

Program description: The new Center, unlike the traditional agency for teenagers has as one of its purposes to provide a range of educational, psychological, medical, and legal services in one place. The two programs are being compared to see how well each has helped the city's youth by, among other things, improving their ego strength.

Step 1: Evaluation question: Do Center participants have better ego strength than participants in the traditional program?

Step 2: Comparisons and hypothesis. A comparison design strategy was used for the evaluation in which participants' ego strength was contrasted in the new and traditional programs. Some 96 participants who were eligible for the new Center and the traditional program participated in the evaluation. A random sampling plan was used to assign them to groups so that 48 participants were assigned to each group. The null hypothesis tested by the analysis was: Participants in the new program and the traditional program have the same ego strength.

Step 3: Getting the data. All individuals who participated in the evaluation were given the River's Ego Strength Inventory, a standardized measure that was accepted as valid and reliable for adolescents. The measure was administered at the end of six months of a person's participation. The highest possible score on the inventory was 75 points, and the lowest possible score was zero.

Step 4: Test the hypothesis and report results.

Descriptive Statistics	
New Program	Traditional Program
$\bar{X}$ = 46.36	$\bar{X}$ = 45.33
SD = 3.46	SD = 3.78
N = 48	N = 48

Source of Variation	Degrees of Freedom (df)	F Value	Level of Significance (p)
New and Traditional Programs	1	3.22	ns (not significant)
Error	94		

The test of the null hypothesis resulted in an F value of 3.22, which is not statistically significant (because the value in the F-statistic table is 3.93552 for 1 and 94 degrees of freedom at the .05 level). Consequently, the hypothesis that participants' ego strength in the new and traditional programs is the same cannot be rejected.

This result was recorded in the evaluator's final report in the following way: A one-way ANOVA was conducted to answer the evaluation question. The analysis was unable to uncover significant differences in average ego strength between teenagers in the Center and traditional program. This suggests that the Center was not better able to improve ego strength.

HOW TO USE THE MANN-WHITNEY U TEST

Statistical methods give formal rules and procedures for testing hypotheses and drawing conclusions about evaluation data. Such procedures are used, for example, to find out if a group taking part in a program is different from its population of origin, or whether one or more groups, some of which took part in a program, are different from one another.

Statistical methods fall into two major categories: parametric and nonparametric. When evaluators have very small samples or data not drawn from normally distributed populations, they usually rely on nonparametric statistics.

Parametric statistical tests are more powerful than nonparametric tests and are based on certain important conditions about the parameters (values) of the population from which the sample comes. Parametric tests use measures from an interval or ratio scale (see

Scaling and Statistics following in this section). Examples of parametric tests include regression and ANOVA.

Nonparametric tests make very minor or no assumptions about the parameters of the population. You can apply such tests to quite small samples using data from any measurement scale—nominal, ordinal, interval, or ratio (explained later in this section).

The Mann-Whitney U Test is one of the most powerful non-parametric techniques. It is used to test for differences between two independent groups, such as two classrooms. It is similar in purpose to the parametric t test, but can be used with ordinal data or when other assumptions of the t test cannot be met.

Here's how one evaluator used the Mann-Whitney test for a small (fewer than 20) sample:

Example 90   Using the Mann-Whitney Test

Barstin Elementary School had ten fourth grade students with severe hearing impairments. Four of the students were in a special program to teach them to speak more clearly. At the end of one semester, the students in the special program (the experimental group) were compared with the six students in the traditional program (the control group).

A special education expert rated each child's ability to speak on a scale from 1 to 20, with 20 representing normal speech. The evaluator tabulated the resulting ratings as follows:

| | Student | | | | | |
	1	2	3	4	5	6
Control	4	7	9	10	12	14
Experimental	8	11	14	15		

If more students had been available, the evaluator might have chosen a t test; but after considering the smallness of the sample size and his unwillingness to make assumptions about populations, the evaluator decided to use the nonparametric Mann-Whitney U test.

How to Compute U

Using the above example, let n_1 be the number of cases in the smaller of the two groups, and let n_2 be the number of cases in the larger of the groups. In this case, $n_1 = 4$ and $n_2 = 6$.

The evaluator tested the null hypothesis that the students in the experimental and control groups received equal ratings. The alternate hypothesis was that the performance of the experimental group students exceeded that of the control group students. (Note that the evaluator used a one-tailed test. A two-tailed test would also have been possible with, for example, the alternate hypothesis that either group exceeded the other.)

The statistic the Mann-Whitney test computes is called U. It represents the number of times a person in the larger group of size n_2 precedes a score in the smaller group of size n_1. For our example, the student ratings lined up as follows:

					Rating				
4	7	8	9	10	11	12	13	14	15
C	C	E	C	C	E	C	C	E	E

Where   E = Experimental group student ($n_1 = 4$)

C = Control group student ($n_2 = 6$)

As you can see from the table, the first control group score (4) is not preceded by any scores from the experimental group. The same is true of the second control group score (7). The third control group score (9) is preceded by one experimental group score (8). The same is true for the fourth score in the control group (10). The last two control group scores (12 and 13) are both preceded by two scores from the experimental group (8 and 11). The U statistic in this case equals the sum of $0 + 0 + 1 + 1 + 2 + 2 = 6$.

Once you have calculated the value of U, you can use a standard table to find out if that value is statistically significant. (You can find tables for nonparametric statistics in some statistical textbooks; we recommend *Nonparametric Statistics for the Behavioral Sciences* by Sidney Siegel, New York, McGraw-Hill, 1956.)

For our example with $n_1 = 4$, $n_2 = 6$ and $U = 6$, the tables will show a statistical significance of $p = .129$. Since most evaluators use $p < .01$ or p < .05 as their criterion of significance, the evaluator probably would conclude that the data do not suggest significant differences between the groups.

Another Way to Compute U

The method used above to compute U is particularly effective when the number of cases in the larger group (n_2) is eight or fewer. The statistical tables for n_2 between 9 and 20 are presented in slightly different form than those for n_2 less than or equal to 8. For values of n_2 up to 20, you may find the following technique more useful.

First, assign ranks to each score in the combined groups. The lowest score gets a rank of 1, and the next lowest score 2, and so on. For tie scores, assign the mean ranking (for example, if two subjects both score 7, and this represents spots 2 and 3 on your ranking scale, assign both scores a rank value of 2.5). You then compute the U statistic as the smaller of the following

$$U_1 = n_1 n_2 + n_1 (n_1 + 1)/2 - R_1$$
or
$$U_2 = n_1 n_2 + n_2 (n_2 + 1)/2 - R_2$$

Where

R_1 = the sum of ranks assigned to the smaller group size n_1

R_2 = the sum of ranks assigned to the larger group size n_2

The following table shows the ranked values, R_1 and R_2, for the data from our example.

Experimental Scores	Rank	Control Scores	Rank
8	3	4	1
11	6	7	2
14	9	9	4
15	10	10	5
	$R_1 = 28$	12	7
		13	8
			$R_2 = 27$

Plugging these data into the preceding equations, you get the following:

$$U_1 = (4)(6) + (4)(4 + 1)/2 - 28 = 6$$

or

$$U_2 = (4)(6) + (6)(6 + 1)/2 - 27 = 18$$

In this case, the smaller of the two is $U_1 = 6$, which is the same value arrived at with statistical tables.

Statistics and Scales

The four common statistical scaling methods are as follows.

Norminal scales give you scores for classifying individuals, objects, or characteristics. Examples include classification according to sex, political affiliation, color of hair, or medical diagnosis. The only meaningful statistics you can compute from nominal scales result from counting and include modes, frequencies, and percentages. Only nonparametric statistical methods can be applied to nominal-scale data.

Ordinal scales classify individuals or objects that stand in some kind of relation to one another, such as relations of preference or quality. Sample ordinal scales are military ranks and grades of meat. The median is the most appropriate statistic derived from ordinal-scale data; nonparametric statistical techniques therefore apply.

Interval scales have all the characteristics of ordinal scales, but the distance between any two points is known. The zero point and the unit of measurement are arbitrary. Take, for example, the measurement of temperature, for which there are two scales, Fahrenheit and Centigrade. The unit of measurement and the zero (freezing) point are different for each scale. Since both scales are linearly related and give the same information, you can use a mathematical formula to convert from one temperature scale to the other. But look at these scales:

Definitely Agree	Probably Agree	No Opinion	Probably Disagree	Definitely Disagree
Excellent	Satisfactory	Average	Fair	Poor

Sometimes such scales are considered ordinal scales, sometimes interval scales; in practice, the evaluator intuitively decides which.

Interval scales can be analyzed using parametric or nonparametric techniques.

Ratio scales, such as height and weight scales, are internal scales with a true zero point. All parametric techniques can be applied to ratio scale data as can nonparametric tests.

HOW TO ANALYZE CATEGORICAL AND CONTINUOUS DATA

A state education department asked an evaluator to find out if the nation's top ten medical schools were accepting the same proportion of students from the two state universities. The evaluator's design looked like this:

School	University	
	Northern State	Southern State
1		
2		
3		
4		
5		
6		
7		
8		
9		
10		

Another evaluator had to find out if the proportion of state university pre-med students being accepted by the best schools was similar to the national average. The evaluator's study design looked like this:

	School									
	1	2	3	4	5	6	7	8	9	10
Frequencies in State										
Frequencies in Nation										

Both evaluators were working with categorical data (in this case, distribution across different schools) as opposed to continuous, or hierarchical, data (for example, ranking the schools accepting students on a scale from 1 to 100). Variables arranged in classes that can be distinguished from one other but cannot be arranged into a hierarchy produce categorical information. For example, classifying sex as male or female or program satisfaction as high or low will produce categorical data.

Chi-Square

The chi-square statistic is a nonparametric technique used to analyze categorical information. Evaluation data often call for two specific procedures that use the chi-square statistic: goodness-of-fit testing and contingency table analysis.

Goodness of fit. Goodness-of-fit testing is a way of comparing empirically derived data (expressed as frequencies) with theoretically expected results. For example, one evaluation question that could be answered using goodness-of-fit testing would be:

How do participants' approval ratings of Program X compare with the one-third disapproval rate of previous years?

Suppose a new demographic theory predicts a certain population will contain four ethnic groups in the proportions 9:3:3:1, and a random sample of 240 persons resulted in 120, 40, 55, and 25 people in the four categories. You can use a goodness-of-fit test to compare the theoretically expected data with the empirically observed data. The result of the test would be a chi-square statistic, which could be computed with the following table and formula:

	Category 1	Category 2	...	Category n
Empirical Frequencies	o_1	o_2	...	o_n
Theoretical Frequencies	t_1	t_2	...	t_n

Chi-square formula:
$$\chi^2 = \sum_{i=1}^{n} \frac{(o_i - t_i)^2}{t_i}$$

where:

n = number of categories

o_i = obtained or empirical frequency for the ith category

t_i = theoretical or expected frequency for the ith category

If the obtained or empirical data (o_i) are the same as the theoretical data (t_i), the fit will be perfect; the difference ($o_i - t_i$) for each category will be zero, and so will the chi-square value. Consequently, the smaller the chi-square value, the better the fit; the larger the chi-square value, the poorer the fit. You can compare your chi-square values with values in chi-square tables and accept or reject the goodness of fit at the desired level of statistical significance.

Contingency tables. Contingency tables are used in chi-square analyses to compare two sets of empirical data expressed as frequencies—for example, in testing for a significant relationship between two variables. The relationship between the proportion of doctors and lawyers and sex might be organized in a contingency table as follows:

	Doctors	Lawyers
Male	Number of Observations	Number of Observations
Female	Number of Observations	Number of Observations

You could also use contingency tables to find out if two sets of empirical data are alike—or, in statistical language, whether the two sets are random samples from the same population. For example, you could use a contingency table and a chi-square statistic to compare the number of children contracting polio in samples of vaccinated and unvaccinated children:

	Not Vaccinated	Vaccinated
Polio	Number of Observations	Number of Observations
No Polio	Number of Observations	Number of Observations

The chi-square statistic used for contingency tables is similar to the one used for goodness-of-fit tests. However, in this case you compare the observed frequencies with expected rather than theoretical frequencies.

Example 91   Chi-Square Analysis

The MEDEX program is designed to help students pass medical school entrance examinations by giving them practice answering typical standardized examination questions. The college's board will approve the MEDEX program if a significantly greater number of MEDEX as opposed to non-MEDEX graduates get accepted by medical school. The evaluation question was, "Is there a statistically significant difference in the rate of medical school acceptance between MEDEX graduates and other students?"

The evaluators used a comparison group design. They organized the data into a contingency table with two variables: program participation and admittance to medical school. They then randomly selected 210 college seniors to take part in the evaluation from all the seniors who requested to enroll in MEDEX. The evaluators randomly accepted half of the 210 students into the program and refused the other half. Two of the refused students were disqualified from the evaluation when they enrolled in another program similar to MEDEX.

Evaluation Sample	
No MEDEX	MEDEX
103	105

The evaluators organized the data into a contingency table and used a chi-square statistic to test the hypothesis that medical school acceptance rates were the same.

	No MEDEX	MEDEX	Totals
Not Admitted	80	30	110
Admitted	23	75	98
Totals	103	105	208

Chi-square value $(\chi^2) = 48.4$

Degrees of freedom $= 1$

Significance $= p < .01$

The results of the chi-square analysis refuted the hypothesis. The evaluators concluded that the chi-square test value of 48.4 indicated a statistically significant difference between MEDEX and non-MEDEX students, with MEDEX students being accepted by medical schools more frequently.

HOW TO USE PATTERN ANALYSIS

Large evaluation projects usually involve data from many different measures. A statewide evaluation of the comparative merit of two dental training programs, for example, might use tests of knowledge, clinical skills, and ability to work with dentists. How can you interpret all this information and decide on the merit of each program? One way is to find statistically significant results consistently favoring one of the two programs. A less reliable, but still acceptable, procedure is to find whether most of the differences favor one program, and then see if this pattern of differences is itself statistically significant. This is called *pattern analysis*.

RZA: A Hypothetical Case Study

The RZA research firm conducted a statewide evaluation of two health maintenance organization (HMOs), each of which was designed to serve persons of all ages and means. HMO A, a new program, emphasized the psychological aspects of care and used new health professionals such as nurse practitioners and physician aides. HMO B offered the traditional health services. RZA had to answer three evaluation questions:

- Is HMO A better then HMO B in improving physical health?
- Is HMO A better than HMO B in promoting good health habits?
- Is HMO A better than HMO B in enhancing mental health?

In the course of RZA's evaluation, all state employees requesting to join an HMO as part of a health benefit package were randomly assigned to one of the two HMOs. The experiment started in 1974. In 1976, and again in 1980, RZA put each participant through a complete battery of tests covering physical health, mental health, and health habits. Each of the tests had several subscales.

The basic design for the evaluation was a time series in which males and females were separately tracked—primarily because each sex traditionally uses health services differently, and in this case, the health

201 Analyzing Information

risks of the males' jobs differed in many instances from the risks associated with the females' jobs. Here is what the design looked like:

Females		Males	
1976	1980	1976	1980

After successfully administering all the measures and getting a 98% response rate in all groups, the RZA evaluators began to analyze the 20 different measures (the physical health and the health habits test batteries each had eight subscales and the mental health battery had four). When the evaluators compared HMO A with HMO B across all the measures in each group (1976 females, 1980 females, 1976 males, and 1980 males) they found very few statistically significant results—although in most cases HMO A seemed to work better than HMO B. Since neither program could meet the criterion of consistent statistically significant differences for each measure, RZA decided to conduct a pattern analysis.

Terms and Tables

Single-group differences. Again, the evaluators had four groups for which they could compare any single measure used in HMO A (the new program) and HMO B (the traditional program). For the pattern analysis, RZA used summary tables to show the *direction* of single-group score differences, rather than to give means and standard deviations. Direction was represented by $A > B$, $B > A$, or $A = B$. This way of presenting findings was less time consuming and also was intuitively meaningful. In addition to showing the differences, RZA's summary tables also showed, with asterisks, whether each difference was statistically significant at the .05 and .01 levels of confidence. For example, a typical table might look like this:

Sample Table

Measure	1976 Females		1980 Females		1976 Males		1980 Males	
	Direction of Difference	Significance	Direction of Difference	Significance	Direction of Difference	Significance	Direction of Difference	Significance
Composite score	A > B	**	A = B		A > B		A > B	*
Score x	A = B		B > A		A > B		A = B	
Score y	A > B		A = B		A = B		A = B	

$*p < .05; **p < .01$

Trends. For each of the 20 measures, the evaluators computed differences for each of the four groups (1976 females, 1980 females, 1976 males, and 1980 males). The evaluators defined a "trend" as follows:

- At least three of four groups must show the same direction (i.e., at least three of the single differences show A > B or B > A); or

- Two groups have the same direction and the other groups do not show the opposite direction (i.e., at least two of the single differences show A > B or B > A and the others show A = B); or

- One group shows statistically significant differences and none of the other groups shows the opposite (i.e., at least one of the single-group differences shows A > B or B > A, this difference is statistically significant at p < .05 or p < .01, and the other differences show A = B).

In the sample table, there was one trend supporting program A (composite score).

The Sign Test[1]

The sign test gets its name from its use of plus and minus signs rather than quantitative metrics. In RZA's evaluation, the evaluators used a plus sign whenever A > B and a minus sign whenever A > B. No signs are assigned to ties.

The null hypothesis tested by the sign test is that the number of plus signs is equal to the number of minus signs. That is, the sign test assesses whether A > B as often as A < B. The null hypothesis is rejected when too few differences of one sign occur.

There are statistical tables for interpreting sign test data. To use them you need to know only the total number of plus and minus signs (labeled N by statisticians), and the number of minus signs (labeled x by statisticians). The columns of the table are arranged by increasing Ns, and the rows by increasing x's. For any given N and x, the entries of the table give the probability or p value. For example, if N = 14 and x = 5, a sign test table will show p = .212. This p value is not significant at p < .05.

But very few statistics texts give a sign table. Fortunately, computing the p value is not too difficult, and you can do it with a hand calculator. The probability of having a certain number of pluses and minuses is based on a mathematical concept called *binomial distribution*. The sign test assumes that the probability of getting a plus or a minus is equal. In this situation, the formula for the binomial distribution can be written as follows:

$$\sum_{x=0}^{x=x'} \binom{N}{x} \left(\frac{1}{2}\right)^N = \sum_{x=0}^{x=x'} \frac{N!}{x!\,(N-x)!} \left(\frac{1}{2}\right)^N$$

Consider the evaluation question on health habits. Evaluators could make 32 single-group comparisons between HMO A and HMO B (8 measures times 4 groups). RZA found that out of 32 comparisons, 20 favored HMO A (20 pluses), 4 favored HMO B (4 minuses), and 8 were ties. They then tested the null hypothesis that the number of pluses and minuses was equal, and the alternative hypothesis was that there were more pluses. In this case, $N = 24$ (the ties are not counted) and $x = x^1 = 4$, and the binomial formula or a table gives $p = .001$ (a significant result). RZA therefore rejected the null hypothesis and suggested that the pattern of differences significantly favored HMO A.

RZA's Findings

Is HMO A better than HMO B in improving physical health? The evaluators had information from eight measures of physical health: minor injuries and illnesses, major injuries and illnesses, doctor visits, hospitalization, costs of treatment (excluding medication), cost of medication, days of work missed because of illness or injury, and a composite score (see Example 92).

Overall, members of HMO A scored better on the physical health measure than did members of HMO B. In the 32 possible comparisons between the groups, HMO A members scored higher in 25 cases, lower in 3 cases, and the same in 4 cases. The evaluators found trends favoring HMO A in all measures except hospitalization and cost of medication. Only four of the differences were statistically significant: 1976 HMO A females scored significantly better than did HMO B females in minor injuries and illnesses, doctor visits, days of work missed, and composite score.

To test the significance of the pattern of differences—which seemed to favor HMO A, even though most differences were not statistically significant—the evaluators computed a sign test, which showed HMO A members did indeed score significantly better than did HMO B members ($p < .01$).

Example 92 Physical Health

Measure	1976 Females Direction of Difference	1976 Females Signifi-cance	1980 Females Direction of Difference	1980 Females Signifi-cance	1976 Males Direction of Difference	1976 Males Signifi-cance	1980 Males Direction of Difference	1980 Males Signifi-cance
Composite score	A > B	**	A > B		A > B		A > B	
Minor illnesses and injuries	A > B	**	A > B		A > B		A > B	
Major illnesses and injuries	A > B		A > B		B > A		A > B	
Doctor visits	A > B	*	A > B		A > B		A > B	
Hospitalization	A > B		B > A		A = B		A > B	
Cost of treatment (excluding medication)	A > B		A = B		A = B		A > B	
Cost of medication	A > B		A = B		B > A		A > B	
Days of work missed because of illness or injury	A > B	*	A > B		A > B		A > B	

*p < .05; **p < .01

205

Example 93   Health Habits

Measure	1976 Females		1980 Females		1976 Males		1980 Males	
	Direction of Difference	Significance	Direction of Difference	Significance	Direction of Difference	Significance	Direction of Difference	Significance
Composite score	A > B		A = B		A > B		A > B	
Drinking	A > B		A > B		A > B	*	A > B	*
Smoking	A = B		A = B		A = B		A = B	
Dental care	A > B		A > B		A > B		A > B	
Diet	A > B	**	A > B		A > B	**	A > B	
Exercise	A > B		B > A		A = B		B > A	
Sleep	A > B		A > B		A > B		A = B	
Safety	A = B		B > A		B > A		A > B	

*p < .05; **p < .01

Example 94 Mental Health

Measure	1976 Females		1980 Females		1976 Males		1980 Males	
	Direction of Difference	Significance	Direction of Difference	Significance	Direction of Difference	Significance	Direction of Difference	Significance
Composite score	A > B	*	A = B		A = B		A > B	
Anxiety/stress	B > A		A = B		B > A	*	B > A	**
Socialization	A > B		A = B		B > A		B > A	
Depression	A = B		A > B		B > A		A > B	

*p < .05; **p < .01

207

Is HMO A better than HMO B in promoting good health habits? There were eight measures of health habits: drinking, smoking, dental care, diet, exercise, sleep, safety, and a composite score (see Example 93).

Once again, the evaluators found few significant single-group differences between programs, but many patterns. Out of 32 tests, 20 differences favored HMO A, and this overall trend was proved significant by the sign test ($p < .01$). In all, the evaluators found five trends. Members of HMO A reported better drinking habits, better dental care habits, better diets, appeared to sleep better, and had higher composite scores. The evaluators found four statistically significant single-group differences favoring HMO A. All these differences related to two measures:

- *drinking* (1976 and 1980 program A males recorded significantly better drinking habits).

- *diet* (1976 program A males and females reported significantly better diets).

Is HMO A better than HMO B in enhancing mental health? RZA studied four measures of mental health: anxiety/stress, socialization, depression, and a composite score. The evaluation findings suggested little difference in mental health between members of the two HMOs (see Example 94).

On the 16 possible differences (four measures times four groups), members of HMO A scored higher in five cases, lower in six cases, and the same in five cases. A sign test showed that the pattern of differences was not significant. The only subpattern the evaluators could discern in the table in Example 94 was a tendency for HMO B males to report better overall mental health than their HMO A counterparts did in 1976.

NOTE

1. The sign test described here is for a situation with approximately 30 or fewer single-group differences of matched pairs.

Writing and Reporting

EVALUATORS NEARLY ALWAYS have to learn how to write proposals for funding and they always have to write reports or present the results of their work orally. In writing and reporting evaluations, several problems are inevitable. In this chapter, we address a few of them.

In the first section, we provide a general but detailed outline of an evaluation report. In the second section, rules for writing are provided, since a perpetual problem is how to convert an explanation of the evaluation into readable English. In the third section of this chapter, we offer ways to help evaluators justify and explain their work by finding references in the literature. It is not uncommon, for example, for potential consumers of evaluation findings or sponsors of studies to expect evaluators to be able to justify their choice of methods, questions, and standards; to compare their activities to those of other evaluators; and to show how the evaluation will either help improve the program being investigated, bring people closer to the program's goals, or contribute some new knowledge about the best ways to improve society.

HOW TO WRITE AN EVALUATION REPORT

The evaluation report is the official record of an evaluation, the document in which you make public your activities and findings. It should be believable, truthful, and easily understood. It's your job to communicate in a comprehensible way—without omitting any qualitative or quantitative details—what was done, how it was done, and why it was done.

A credible evaluation report clearly and logically describes the evaluation questions and the procedures you used to get the answers. It should include:

- an introduction to the evaluation, the evaluation questions, and limitations on the scope of the evaluation;
- the design strategy and the sampling procedures for each evaluation question, and their limitations;
- the information collection techniques and instruments and their limitations, and any field activities;
- the methods you used to analyze the evaluation information, their limitations, and the results for each analysis;
- the answers to each evaluation question, including your interpretation of the findings and your recommendations; and
- administrative details such as schedules and staff assignments.

The Introduction

In the introduction, you should briefly describe the program or programs being evaluated, the group that is conducting the evaluation, and your approach to evaluation. Discuss any legislation that created the program and mandated its evaluation. Be sure to include the process you (and your client) used to arrive at statements of program goals, activities, and evidence of program merit. Finally, explain your choice of evaluation questions, list the questions, and describe any constraints imposed upon the scope of the evaluation.

Reporting Design and Sampling

Here you should describe the evaluation's design strategy and sampling procedures and any limitations on them. For each evaluation question, explain and justify the way you grouped participants, the independent and dependent variables, the sample, and any limitations on internal and external validity. A drawing of the design is also helpful.

Include the sampling procedure you used (e.g., random sampling); justify any subdivisions or strata into which you divided potential participants for sampling purposes; show the final numbers of individuals in the sample; and explain any problems you encountered in selecting the participants or any limitations that are inherent in the sampling plan. Again, a drawing of the final sample is useful.

Finally, discuss how well the procedures you used produced the desired sample, at least as far as you can tell with statistical methods or comparisons with tables of demographic data.

Here's an example of one way to report sample and design information:

Example 95   Reporting Sample and Design Information

The sample. The Kennedy Unified School District, the largest district in the state, was selected to participate in the evaluation. In each of the district's 32 elementary schools, one third-grade classroom was selected at random for the experimental health program, and one third-grade classroom was selected at random not to receive any health education program. The remaining classrooms were allowed to continue with their regular health education program, if one existed. The sample is depicted in the following figure.

	School 1	School 2	...	School 32	Total
	The Evaluation Sample				
Experimental Program	1 classroom	1 classroom	...	1 classroom	32 classrooms
No Program (Control)	1 classroom	1 classroom	...	1 classroom	32 classrooms
Total	2 classrooms	2 classrooms	...	2 classrooms	64 classrooms

The sample selected to participate in the evaluation was compared to all third-grade students in Kennedy Unified School District in terms of students' age, reading and general scholastic ability, and ethnic and sex composition, and teachers' years of experience, sex, and ethnicity. The results of a series of chi-square tests showed that there were no significant differences between the sample and all third-grade students.

The design. The design strategy used to group students is described separately for each evaluation question.

Evaluation Question 4: Did students in the experimental program know significantly more about diseases at the end of the school year then they did at the beginning?

To answer the question, a time-series design was used. The independent variable was the timing of measures (which was studied at two levels: preinstruction and postinstruction) and the dependent variable was knowledge of diseases. All classrooms in the experimental program were included in the design, which can be illustrated as follows:

Preinstruction	Postinstruction

The limitations on the internal validity of the design include history (some event like the public television series on the microbe hunters might have influenced students' knowledge); maturation (during the school year students may have matured and in so doing, may have learned more about their bodies' health and disease); testing (taking the preinstruction measure may have affected students' performance on the postinstruction measure, although different forms of the measures were used on each occasion); and instrumentation (the administration procedures may have differed from time to time).

Limitations on the design's external validity include the reactive effects of testing (the preinstruction measure may have alerted students to their lack of knowledge about diseases, making them more attentive to the program); the interactive effects of selection bias (students in this program may not be representative of students in other districts); the reactive effects of innovation (the fact that students were in a special program might have motivated them to learn); multiple program interference (some of the students also participated in a compensatory education program at the same time as the health education program, and it was not possible to distinguish the effects of one program from the other).

Reporting Information Collection

Describe each instrument, the people to whom it was administered and when, and explain why you chose that particular instrument for answering the evaluation questions. Reprint the entire instrument if possible. If not, give sample items. If the instrument has been commercially published and is protected by copyright, you may have to settle for giving instructions about how to order a copy.

Give information about the reliability and validity of the instruments. Were they pilot tested or validated? If so, with whom and by whom? What were the results? It's also a good idea to explain how the instruments were administered and scored.

Summarize all field activities, noting any irregularities in information collection activity, tell how many you obtained complete data for, and explain any missing information.

Here's an example of one way to report information collection:

Example 96   Reporting Information Collection

Information collection. For each question, the evaluation team selected one or more information collection techniques that were likely to provide answers. The proposed information collection techniques were submitted to the Advisory Committee for review. The table on p. 214 contains an excerpt from the approved Evaluation Questions with Information Collection Techniques document and summarizes any limitations.

The Evaluation Questions with Information Collection Techniques

Evaluation Questions	Information Collection Technique(s) To Be Used	Schedule	Limitations: Design	Limitations: Sampling	Limitations: Other
1.					
2.					
3.					
4. Did students in the experimental program know significantly more about diseases at the end of the school year than they did at beginning?	Paper and Pencil Achievement Test		Must have parallel forms of the achievement test	All program participants must be tested	Must insure confidentiality of responses
5.					
6.					

Once the information collection techniques were agreed upon, the evaluation team began to select, adapt, or develop the appropriate instruments. Each of these instruments will now be discussed.

To answer the question about students' knowledge of diseases, the evaluation team chose the New Health Achievement Test (NHAT) because it was specifically designed to measure elementary school students' knowledge of health problems and how to manage them. The NHAT was developed by the National Institute for Health Education and is available from them. The NHAT is a self-administered test and takes approximately 30 minutes for students to complete.

This instrument has been validated on over 6000 elementary school children within the last five years. Split-half reliability of .89 and test/retest reliability of .98 were reported on the average for third-grade students. Content validity was established through expert review by over 100 educators and health professionals.

Reporting Information Analysis

Describe the relationship of each separate analytic method to the evaluation questions, the source of information for the analysis, the design strategy (including the independent and dependent variables), and any limitations. Give the analysis results and interpret the findings related to the evaluation questions for each analytic procedure. Finally, although you need not explain their mathematical or philosophical derivations, the analyses must be named and justified. No matter how careful an evaluator you are, the quality of your methodology may be challenged because there are many equally appropriate procedures, each with its own advocates.

The Evaluation Findings

The most critical part of any evaluation report is the answers to the evaluation questions. You must provide clear and succinct answers or describe the progress you are making toward obtaining them. When reporting answers to evaluation questions, it's important to point out both the strengths and the weaknesses of the program. Clients who have been involved in the program are likely to reject findings that are totally negative. Others are likely to be suspicious if an evaluation report is totally favorable. Occasionally, of course, you may have only positive or negative findings to report.

Recommendations sometimes accompany answers to evaluation questions, but not all clients ask for or want recommendations. You should always find out in advance whether recommendations are required, and if they are, how extensive they should be. When making recommendations, don't take on the policymaker's responsibility for deciding whether or not to continue a program's funding. Instead, you should focus on how to improve the program, on changes that might achieve better results, and on the people who are most likely to benefit from the program.

It's important to explain the limitations of the evaluation. If information came from instruments whose reliability or validity is suspect, tell the reader about it when the evaluation question is answered. You must report the limitations on your findings even if this makes the report appear noncommittal and the results more difficult to translate into action. Your responsibility is to give policymakers credible and understandable answers they can use to make decisions.

Reporting Administration

Explain the sequence of events between defining the evaluation questions and arriving at the answers. Information about you and your staff may also be appropriate in this section of the report.

One way you can combine information about the evaluation schedule and the staff is to draw up a calendar of events. Here's an example:

Example 97   Evaluation Schedule

October 19, 1980	Meeting with Dr._____ and others from the Office of _____ ....
October 31, 1980	Proposed for Evaluation Study of _____ submitted to the Office of _____ ....
November 20, 1980	Revised evaluation design submitted to Dr. _____ at the District Office of _____ ....
June 30, 1981	Sampling procedures refined and implemented ....
July 31, 1982	Data analysis completed ....
August 15, 1982	Preliminary draft of final report completed ....
August 31, 1982	Submission of Final Report to State Department of Health, Education and Welfare ....
September 1, 1982	Thank you letter sent to all participants in the evaluation study ....

The Evaluation Summary

Evaluation summaries distill into a few pages the activities and findings described in a relatively large evaluation report. The purpose of the summary is to give people an overview of the evaluation that is easy to read but detailed enough to be believable and usable. Sometimes the summary is placed at the beginning of an evaluation report as a kind of introduction. Because it may be more widely read and circulated than the complete report, prepare your evaluation summary carefully. Use professional writers or editors if funds permit.

HOW TO IMPROVE YOUR WRITING

> I keep six honest serving men
> (They taught me all I knew):
> Their names are What and Why and When
> and How and Where and Who.

Perhaps you remember this verse from Rudyard Kipling. It is still used to remind students how to make their essays clear and understandable. Not all evaluators, however, recall all the rules of writing. Nevertheless, evaluators do a great deal of writing. In this section, four additional "serving men" are discussed that, when used properly, can enhance the quality of evaluation reports, but when used improperly, make them clumsy and obscure. They are: the verb *to be*, prepositions, conjunctions, and pronouns.

To Be

Verbs express action. In the sentence, *He hit the ball*, a subject (he) performs the action (hit) to the object (ball). When the sentence reads, *He was hit by the ball*, the subject is not performing the action but receives it. When the subject is the actor, the verb is in the active voice; when the subject is the receiver, the verb is in the passive voice. The passive voice always includes some form of the verb *to be*.

To be stands apart from other verbs because it does not suggest action. It may serve as an auxiliary and enter into a compound verb form as it does in helping to describe a progression. *He was walking* is quite different from *He walked*. *To be* also serves as a link, joining the subject to its complement. In the sentence, *He is tall*, the subject is linked to an adjective; in the sentence, *He is the author*, the subject is linked to a noun.

Among the leading causes of hard-to-read evaluations is the misuse of *to be*; many writers rely heavily on its function as a link and in the passive voice. Consider this:

> *Poor:* This report *is* an excellent summary of current concepts of evaluation. It *is* profusely illustrated with case examples and clear tables and figures. The text *is* relatively simple and *is* obviously written for the nonexpert for there *are* very few references cited.

These three sentences contain five verbs; in all of them some form of *to be* appears, twice as a link and three times as an auxiliary in passive verbs.

Try this:

> *Better:* Profusely illustrated with case examples, clear tables, and figures, this small monograph summarizes excellently the current concepts of evaluation. The relatively simple text is obviously written for the nonexpert, for it cites very few references.

These sentences have three verbs, two of them active and one passive, and no links at all. This is an improvement over the first version, having fewer words and more action. To arrive at this better version, some guidelines have been followed. First, the adjective has been connected directly to the subject, eliminating an *is:* Instead of *The text is relatively simple,* say, *The relatively simple text.* Second, a noun complement has been converted into a verb: *is a summary* becomes *summarizes:* This small monograph summarizes current concepts. (Once that was done, the *excellent* that originally modified summary was made into the adverb *excellently,* and another *is* was removed with *of.*)

To help with the passive, turn the original subject into the grammatical object. *There are very few references cited* turns into *cites very few references.* What then becomes the subject? Who or what cites? Obviously, the text. Since the word *text* has already occurred (in the main clause), the pronoun *it* can be used (in the subordinate): *for it* [the text] *cites very few references.*

A rule of thumb for evaluators is that in any segment of writing, no more than one-fourth to one-third of the verbs should be passive or links. For example, you could take eight to ten consecutive sentences from a report and count the number of verbs. Record this denominator as a fraction. Then count the passive and links as the numerator. If the fraction exceeds one-third, you have too many.

Prepositions

Prepositions show relationships between terms. One device used to help remember the words that are prepositions is to think of what a plane can do to a cloud: go *under, over, through, near, by,* and so on. When a sentence has too many prepositions, it can get unwieldy and confusing. Consider this:

> *Poor:*   There had been major changes *in* the speech related *to* the data accumulated *as* a consequence *of* exhaustive study *of* the results *of* participation *in* preschool programs.

This sentence has a single verb in the passive, 27 words, and seven prepositions! Here's how it might be improved:

> *Better:*   The author changed her speech after she had exhaustively studied the results *of* participation *in* preschool programs. (17 words, 2 verbs in the active voice, and 2 prepositions)

Here's what was done. First, the passive was changed into the active (*The author changed her speech*); next, unnecessary prepositions were deleted (*as a consequence of exhaustive study of* becomes *exhaustively studied*). Some guidelines for reducing the number of prepositions are:

- Delete an entire prepositional phrase when it adds nothing to the meaning: *in order to provide the answer* means no more than *to provide the answer.*

- Convert a prepositional phrase to a participle. *In the attempt to validate the instruments* can become *attempting to validate the instruments.*

- Convert a prepositional phrase to an adjective: *It is a question of importance* becomes *It is an important question.*

- Change the passive voice to the active: *The grades were determined by the students* can become *The students determined the grades.*

Conjunctions

Conjunctions join two or more words, phrases, or clauses. One class is the coordinating conjunction: *and, but, or.* These join two terms of equal grammatical standing:

- We conducted the evaluation *and* they reported the results.
- The students *and* the teachers participated in the evaluation.
- The students wrote reports *and* took tests.
- We varied the praise *and* blame.
- The teacher lectured slowly to the parents *and* students.

A second class of conjunctions is the subordinating: *if, as, when, because.* This class shows grammatical inequality.

> The data collectors will conduct interviews *if* they get permission from parents.

The main clause, *The data collectors will conduct interviews* can stand on its own. The dependent clause, *if they get permission from parents,* cannot, and thus, it is considered grammatically unequal or subordinate.

Although by no means alone in being misused, the conjunction *and* is among the evaluator's major targets. *And* should connect terms that are grammatically similar, that is, exhibit a parallel construction.

Poor: He conducted and reported the results of a four-year evaluation.

Better: He conducted a four-year evaluation and reported its results.

Poor: Drs. Smith and Jones have written an excellent book on the use of statistics in evaluations which probably far surpasses and is unlike any other treatise on the subject.

Better: Drs. Smith and Jones have written an excellent book on the use of statistics in evaluations, which probably far surpasses any other treatise on the subject.

Even Better: In their excellent book on the use of statistics in evaluation, Drs. Smith and Jones have written a treatise that probably far surpasses any other on the subject.

Pronouns

All pronouns refer to an antecedent, usually a noun (or pronoun), called a referrent. Two problems are associated with the use of pronouns: overuse and unclear referrents. Look at this example.

> *It* is a natural impulse, when the manuscript is completed, to put *it* in an envelope and mail *it* to the editor.

In this sentence, the first *it* is called an anticipatory subject since it anticipates the rest of the sentence and has no clear referrent; the second *it* refers to the manuscript. But to what does the third *it* refer? The envelope or the manuscript? As a practical matter, the reference makes little difference since the manuscript is in the envelope, and when you mail one, you automatically mail the other. But, the sentence may be confusing. Try this:

> *Poor:* Any proposed idea needs constant evaluation and revision. *It* is only in this way that *it* can be useful.

The first *it* is anticipatory, but the second is a relative pronoun whose reference is unclear (idea? evaluation? revision? way?). Between the intended referrent, *idea*, and the *it* are three nouns. To find the reference, the reader must skip over these and go back to a noun far removed from the pronoun. The sentence could be helped by removing the anticipatory *it*, but even then, the problem of the second *it* remains. A better way to recast the two sentences is:

> Any proposed idea needs constant testing and revision, which alone can make it useful.

Here is another example.

> *Poor:* This represented a challenge to our mature values that had to be eliminated as soon as possible.

> *Better:* This challenge to our mature values had to be eliminated as soon as possible.

Summary

Here are some guidelines for writing evaluation reports more clearly:

(A) *To improve use of the verb "to be":*
  • connect the adjective directly to the subject.

- convert the noun complement to a verb.

- turn the subject into the grammatical object.

(B) *To improve use of prepositions:*
  - delete prepositions that are unnecessary.

  - convert prepositional phrases into participles.

  - convert prepositional phrases into adjectives.

  - change the passive voice to the active.

(C) *To improve use of conjunctions:*
  - when using *and* make sure you are connecting terms that are grammatically equal.

(D) *To improve use of pronouns:*
  - make sure the referrent is clear.

  - avoid using too many in any given segment of your writing.

HOW TO SEARCH FOR EVALUATION REFERENCES

Have you ever set out to write an evaluation proposal or a report of your activities, only to discover you weren't really sure how many others had been involved in similar projects, what instruments they used, or even whether their projects had been successful?

Evaluators are frequently called upon to describe the framework of knowledge for their work, to justify their methods and evaluation standards, to compare their activities with others, and to explain what their project will contribute to the field. That usually means going to published and unpublished sources to find out what already exists in the field. But what used to take a few hours on the telephone or in the college library has become much more complicated.

Today you must contend with a vast and rapidly proliferating array of documents about how people think, feel, behave, and learn. To ensure credibility, you also have to demonstrate that you understand a wide range of topics, like the availability and financial aspects of services in other states and countries.

When to Collect Reference Information

Most Requests for Proposals (RFPs) for evaluation studies require bidders to convince the reviewers that they know the field. In fact, for some RFPs, the "contractor's demonstrated knowledge" of the subject is worth 10% or more in determining who gets a grant or contract. "Is the evaluator knowledgeable about the strategies and results of other similar evaluations?" the reviewers seem to be asking.

Even if you never compete for a grant or contract, you will always have to reassure someone that you have mastered your field, that you will be using the most up-to-date and accurate methods available, and that you will not "reinvent the wheel."

Here are some occasions when you might want to use a reference review:

- *To introduce or describe the evaluation and its significance.* Tell the audience what other programs exist, why this one should be evaluated, and how your evaluation will provide new or better information.

- *To justify your choice of evaluation questions or hypotheses.* When appropriate, you should tell your audience about the background information on which you have based your assumptions. Why were those questions asked, for example, and not some others that may also be important?

- *To establish evaluation standards.* It helps to tell the evaluation audience about existing criteria for achievement obtained in the past that might be worth striving for today. For example, have similar programs achieved statistically significant gains among groups? Have other programs improved outcomes by 20%? By more than 20%?

- *To support the choice of evaluation methods.* If you are using a particular model of evaluation practice, then it's probably a good idea to justify it and explain why you used that model and not some other. Is it the most practical? The most technically sound? You should also explain the choice of designs, instruments, and analytical techniques. Are the measures reliable? Are they valid? How was their selection made?

Here's a hypothetical example of how to use references to enhance your written evaluations:

Evaluation Question 1: Is pain controlled more effectively in terminal patients under hospice care than in those under other types of management?

Criteria: A cardinal principle of terminal care is the alleviation of suffering (AAHC, 1972). Many terminally ill patients have malignant diseases with the associated symptoms of weakness, anorexia, constipation, nausea, and pain.

Pain is the most prevalent symptom in cancer patients (who comprise 90% of all hospice populations) and the most feared (Lewis, 1975). Clinical studies have shown that medical personnel often undertreat pain (Martin and Sachac, 1973). Hospices have evolved a medical approach to the treatment of the chronic pain associated with terminal illness by giving high doses of potent analgesics, sometimes in combination with psychotropic agents, on a regular schedule, never waiting for the patient to ask for pain relief (Melzack and Mounter, 1976). This aggressive approach has been assessed in studies at Good Samaritan Hospital which revealed that only 8% of hospice patients have unrelieved pain five days after admission compared to over 30% of these same patients before admission (Lipson, 1975). The Royal Canadian Hospice Association has reported the effective use of Brompton's mixture (a mixture of a variable amount of diamorphine, 10 mg of cocaine, 2.5 ml of ethyl alcohol, and chloroform in water), and found that pain was relieved in 90% of their hospice patients compared to 75% to 80% of the patients in the rest of the hospital (Kane, 1977).

The criterion we will apply to the interpretation of evaluation question 1 is that fewer than 10% of hospice patients will, at any time, have "intolerable" pain (as defined by the Good Samaritan Pain Scale). We also expect that statistically significantly fewer hospice than comparison patients will report "mostly unrelieved" pain. To prevent the purchase of pain relief at the expense of mental clarity (Fross and Plaut, 1976), we will observe whether more hospice patients are classified as confused or disoriented than other patients.

Where to Find References

Many government and private agencies that sponsor evaluations have past reports of a program's accomplishments and the findings of other, perhaps similar, programs. Some of the health agencies, for example, the American Cancer Society or the American Lung Association, sometimes have available to the public written information in the form of books, reports, and pamphlets. Further, public libraries might stock periodicals and books that are relevant to a particular evaluation study. The major sources of information, however, are university and college libraries, especially if they have associated with them medical, nursing, or education schools or have training programs for other health professionals like social workers, dieticians, occupational therapists, and so on.

Access to information on library shelves is typically made by using the card catalog. Suppose you are the evaluator for a program whose overall goal is to improve the quality of medical care for the elderly. To justify your choice of evaluation standards, you might recall that the National Commission on the Aged had once been concerned with criteria for care. Thus, by looking in the card catalog, you might find the following:

```
WT        National Commission on the Aged
30
N2135     Standards of care for older people ... .
 1953
          Contents V.I.   Suggested standards for homes
          for the aged; nursing homes.

          V.2.   Methods of establishing and maintaining
          standards

          V. 3.   Bridging the gap between existing
          practices and desirable goals in homes for
          the aged and nursing homes.
```

The call number at the top left of the card is derived from the Library of Congress system, which has replaced the Dewey Decimal System in most large libraries.

One great convenience to the evaluator is access to computer reference searches. The computer will enable you to identify the most current sources of information on almost any topic in health, and it can save you a great deal of effort.

Examples of computer data bases that may be of special use to evaluators are:

- American Statistics Index
- Bioethics Line (legal and ethical health-related issues included in the *Bibliography of Bioethics*)
- Congressional Information Service
- ERIC Federal Register Abstracts
- MEDLINE (1977); Backfiles 1966-1976 (Biomedical literature included in the *Index Medicus, Index to Dental Literature, International Nursing Index,* and *Hospital Literature Index*)
- New York *Times* Information Bank
- NTIS (National Technical Information Service; corresponds to Government Reports Announcements and Weekly Government Abstracts)
- SSIE (latest two years: description of research projects in progress in physical, medical, life, and social sciences from the Smithsonian Science Information Exchange)
- Toxline: (Toxicologic and pharmacologic information on drugs, industrial chemicals, and environmental pollutants)

Two Computerized Data Bases: MEDLINE and ERIC

MEDLINE is an online bibliographic search service designed by the National Library of Medicine to provide rapid access to current literature. The MEDLINE data base consists of citations to articles from over 3000 journals indexed for Index Medicus, Index to Dental Literature, International Nursing Index, and Hospital Literature Index (starting in 1978). In addition, papers and chapters from selected congresses, symposia, proceedings, and multi-author monographs have been included since May 1976. The MEDLINE data base is designed to be a two- to three-year file of the most recent literature.

Citations are retrieved from the data bases by coordinating appropriate search terms such as subject headings (taken from Medical Subject Headings), authors, and languages. These terms are put into search statements using Boolean logic (*and*, *or*, and *not*) to describe the subject of the search. Search statements are entered on a typewriter-like terminal, which is connected to the National Library of Medicine's computer via a telecommunication system. Citations to articles that match the specific requirements are retrieved while the librarian is at the terminal. These citations can then be printed immediately if the bibliography is 25 citations or less. Larger bibliographies are printed offline and mailed from the National Library of Medicine to the searcher.

A MEDLINE printout lists references, each containing author (AU), title (TI), and journal or paper source (SO), as illustrated below. In addition, author abstracts (AB) are included for many citations indexed since 1975:

AU—McDonnel DF

TI —Pineal epidermoid cyst: its surgical therapy

AB—A pineal epidermoid cyst was initially diagnosed as a pinealoma. Seven years later combined computerized axial tomography and carotidvertabral angiography accurately delineated the location and suggested the diagnosis of this histologically benign lesion. Microsurgical technique via a right occipital transtentorial approach allowed successful intracapsular resection of this tumor.

SO—Surg Neurol 7(6): 387-391, June 1977

The cost of these searches will undoubtedly vary. They include the library's charges for telecommunication and offline printing costs. A realistic set of costs might range from $7.00 to $22.00, depending on the number of years covered and whether you want both citations and abstracts or just citations only.

ERIC may be the most important data base for evaluators of education programs. ERIC is a decentralized, nationwide information system operated through the National Institute of Education for the purpose of providing ready access to descriptions of exemplary programs, research and development efforts, and related information that can be used in developing more effective educational programs. Through a network of specialized clearinghouses, information is monitored, acquired, evaluated, indexed, and abstracted for inclusion in monthly reference products and other publications.

Information from the clearinghouses is sent to the computerized record, which is used to produce *Resources in Education*, the monthly abstract journal. Copies of the original documents are available for sale on microfiche and in hardcopy reproduction.

What are the principal tools for using ERIC?

- *Resources in Education* (RIE), called *Research in Education* prior to January 1975, is a monthly indexing and abstracting journal that announces research reports, critiques, bibliographies, field studies, directories, and other documents from various sources.

- *Current Index to Journals in Education* (CIJE) is a monthly annotated index to more than 700 publications representing the core periodical literature in the field of education.

- *Thesaurus of ERIC Descriptors* is a collection of more than 8000 terms (descriptors) that serve as the indexing vocabulary used to describe the various reports, projects, and journal articles entered into the ERIC system. Descriptors are derived from documents and journal articles in the ERIC program.

To use ERIC with the help of a computer:

- Prepare a clear and concise statement of the problem or of the information need.

- Determine the nature of the information need and the type of record of publication you should consult (e.g., an ERIC document or a journal citation).

- Using the *Thesaurus of ERIC Descriptors* to identify the terms (subject headings) describing the problem:

   —Look up topics in the Descriptor List to determine whether they are used as ERIC descriptors. If not, a cross-reference may direct you to a synonym, (e.g., Occupation Training USE VOCATIONAL EDUCATION);

   —scan the array of related descriptors listed below each main term (in boldface type) to be sure that you have selected the most specific terms to describe your ends; or

   —use the "Rotated Descriptor Display" to discover the use of key topics, such as VISUALLY HANDICAPPED, and proceed to the Descriptor List to note any closely related terms.

Example 98 shows an ERIC printout.

Example 98   An ERIC Printout

DIALOG File1: ERIC 66-79/FEB (Item   29 of   53) User9002 30may79

ED103314
    Selected Topics in Non-Formal Education. Bibliographies in
Non-Formal Education, Number 3.
    Colletta, Nat J.
    Michigan State Univ., East Lansing. Inst. for International
Studies in Education.
    17p.; Related documents are ED 068 428 and SO 008 170   71
    EDRS Price MF–$0.76   HC–$1.58 PLUS POSTAGE

ED100772
    Non-Formal Education in Ethiopia. Program of Studies in
Non-Formal Education. Team Reports.
    Niehoff, Richard O.; Wilder, Bornard D.
    Michigan State Univ., East Lansing. Inst. for International
Studies in Education.
    358p.; For related documents, see SO 008 058-064   74
    EDRS Price MF–$0.76   HC–$18.40 PLUS POSTAGE

ED090489
    The Worldwide Right to Read.
    Holloway, Ruth Love
    23p.; Paper delivered before the Fourth World Congress on
Reading, Buenos Aires, Argentina Aug 72
    EDRS Price MF–$0.76   HC–$1.58 PLUS POSTAGE

ED085690#
    Research in the Fields of Reading and Communications.
    Lohrer, Alice, Ed.
    Illinois Univ., Urbana. Graduate School of Library Science.
    Library Trends, v22 n2 Entire Issue October 1973
    251p. Oct 73
    Univ. of Illinois Press, Urbana, Ill. 61801 ($2.50)
    Document Not Available from EDRS.

ED083332
    Oral vs. Written Presentations of Industrial Acculturation
Materials to Unemployed Black Males. Illinois Studies of the
Economically Disadvantaged, Technical Report Number 19,
August, 1973.
    Rissman, A. Kent; Jaccard, James J.
    Illinois Univ., Urbana. Dept. of Psychology.
    35p. Aug 73
    EDRS Price MF–$0.76   HC–$1.95 PLUS POSTAGE

Finding Key Words to Describe the Problem

Perhaps the most important skill you need to use MEDLINE or ERIC or other computerized data systems is the ability to identify key words or descriptors that summarize an evaluation problem. You should describe the problem as specifically as possible, and define any terms that have special meanings. If there are points not to be included, you should state those, too.

Suppose you were interested in finding educational programs and products for training professionals in health and other fields to care for the elderly. You might describe your problem to MEDLINE or ERIC this way:

> Post-secondary educational programs and products on acute, inter-mediate, and long-term care for the elderly in community and institutional programs (print and nonprint media) designed to train professionals like teachers, psychiatrists, internists, family practi-tioners, neurologists, physical therapists, occupational therapists, nutritionists, pharmacists, social scientists, nurses, psychologists, podiatrists, social workers, dentists, and osteopaths.

SELECTED BIBLIOGRAPHY

During the past decade, program evaluation has become an established field of study with its own vocabulary and literature. Still, if you want to learn about evaluation or contribute new knowledge to the field, it is often difficult to know where to go. One reason is that evaluation theory and practice have been derived from many other fields, such as education, psychology, sociology, and health. To study evaluation, you generally have to search the books and journals of many disciplines. This bibliography contains references that we have found to be useful.

GENERAL REFERENCES

Abt, C. C. [ed.] *The evaluation of social programs.* Beverly Hills, CA; Sage, 1976.

The book includes papers and discussions from a conference on Social Programs Evaluation held in Cambridge, Massachusetts, in September 1974. The book is divided into seven parts: Part I—Evaluation of Social Experiments—offers a survey and examples of several major social experiments; Part II—Policy Research, Decisions, and Political Impacts of Evaluation Research—discusses the policy effects; Part III—Payoffs of Evaluation Research—emphasizes that evaluation must meet many different criteria to be useful; Part IV—Research versus Decision Requirements and Best Practices of Evaluation—is concerned with why evaluations so often produce negative results; Part V—Evaluation of Health Programs—and Part VI—Evaluation of Education Programs—present examples and issues specific to evaluations in those two areas. In conclusion, Part VII—Research Allocation Strategies deals with ways to improve the allocation of resources.

Caro, F. G. [ed.] *Readings in evaluation research* (2nd. ed.). New York: Russell Sage, 1977.

In the second edition of this well-known book, the editor brings together material from a wide variety of sources. This, he notes, is because social research methods used in evaluation fall between traditional disciplines and a number of applied social science fields. Includes a broad review of evaluation research writings.

Cronbach, L. J. and Associates. *Toward reform of program evaluation.* San Francisco: Jossey-Bass, 1980.

According to the authors, the mission of evaluation is to "facilitate a democratic pluralistic process by enlightening all participants." They also present in easy to assimilate form 95 theses about the purposes of evaluation, the relationship between evaluation and policy research, the lack of wisdom in focusing on whether a project has attained its goals, and the beliefs that the evaluator is an educator.

Fink, A. and J. Kosecoff. *An evaluation primer.* Beverly Hills, CA: Sage, 1978.

Discusses the fundamentals necessary to conduct and interpret evaluations of social programs. Each chapter explains how to perform a specific evaluation activity and offers a number of examples drawn from actual experience. In addition, two workbooks—one focusing on education and one on health—provide exercises to practice evaluation skills. Each of seven chapters covers one major aspect of an evaluation: formulating evaluation questions, constructing evaluation designs, planning and collecting evaluation information, conducting data analysis, reporting, and managing an evaluation.

Guttentag, M. and E. T. Struening. [eds.] *Handbook of evaluation research* (Vol. 2). Beverly Hills, CA: Sage, 1975.

The second volume of the *Handbook of Evaluation Research* focuses on evaluations in several areas, their special problems, and the relevant evaluation methodologies. Part I is a preface by the editors; Part II—Politics and Values in Evaluation Research—discusses the political, ethical, and human aspects of evaluating human service programs; Part III—Cost Benefit Approach to Evaluation—discusses methods and critical analysis of cost-benefit and cost-effectiveness; Part IV—Evaluation of Mental Health Programs—analyzes important aspects of evaluation of mental health programs; Part V—Selected Content Areas in Evaluation Research—presents methodologies in early childhood, public health, and new careers. The volume concludes with a cumulative bibliography.

Isaac, S., M. Isaac, B. William. *Handbook in research and evaluation.* San Diego CA: EDITS, 1971.

This is a concise summary of basic research and evaluation methods drawn from key sources. It provides an overview of relevant methodologies, an exhibit of models, and a listing of their respective strengths and weaknesses. By design, the handbook is oversimplified and requires supplementary texts in the field. The five chapters are: (1) Planning Research and Evaluation Studies; (2) Guide to Research Designs, Methods, and Strategies; (3) Instrumentation and Measurement; (4) Statistical Techniques and the Analysis of Data; and (5) Criteria and Guidelines for Planning, Preparing, Writing, and Evaluating the Research Proposal, Report, Thesis or Article.

Mason, E. J. and W. J. Bramble. *Understanding and conducting research: Applications in education and the behavioral sciences.* New York: McGraw-Hill, 1978.

Explains the fundamentals of research methodology for readers examining issues for the first time. Covers all major aspects of a research activity. Gives extensive attention to measurement, design, and statistics, with an attempt made to treat these concepts as tools, rather than goals, of research. Emphasizes the ability to recognize relevant research questions and problems. Includes a broad introduction to science and research, discussing causality and reasoning, modes of research investigation, and formulation of research problems and hypotheses. Explores all three types of research design: preexperimental, true experimental, and quasi-experimental, with practical, as well as theoretical, issues. Deals with the basic issues and concerns in evaluation research, introduces research statistics, and discusses measurement and observation. Offers guidelines for writing research reports and proposals, and discusses the computer's role in research. The book concludes with some perspectives and speculations on research.

Meyers, W. A. *The evaluation enterprise.* San Francisco, CA: Jossey-Bass, 1981.

This book, written for evaluators, combines much new and important material. Among the most interesting are discussions of the management of evaluations (which is concerned with clients' needs); the advantages and limitations of the objectives-based approach; how to apply managerial and administrative tools (like cost-benefit analysis); and the controversies over quantitative and qualitative methods.

Reicken, H. W. and R. F. Boruch. [eds.] *Social experimentation: A method for planning and evaluating social intervention.* New York: Academic, 1974.

The product of a committee appointed by the Social Science Research Council in 1971, this book summarizes knowledge about how to use randomized experiments in planning and evaluating social programs. While the authors strongly endorse true experimentation as a methodology, they do not advocate its exclusive use. The book covers the nature of social experimentation—its advantages, limitations, and practical possibilities; the major scientific and technical issues in measurement, design, and analysis; problems confronting managers of experiments in the field—negotiating objectives, preserving the integrity of the design, collecting data, and disseminating the findings. The final chapters deal with important institutional and political factors in social experimentation and the issues of confidentiality and ethics. An appendix lists references to abstracts of randomized experiments for appraising a wide variety of social programs.

Rossi, P. H. and H. E. Freeman. *Evaluation: A systematic approach* (2nd ed.). Beverly Hills, CA: Sage, 1982.

A comprehensive, up-to-date introductory textbook. Perhaps its most important contribution is the integration of economic evaluation approaches (cost-benefit and cost-effectiveness analysis) with evaluation study design and data collection procedures from the other social sciences. Presented in the task-oriented framework of program planning and evaluation.

Shortell, S. M. and W. C. Richardson. *Health program evaluation.* St. Louis, MO: C. V. Mosby, 1978.

Although the purpose of this book is to present major concepts, methodologies, and issues in the evaluation of health services programs, it is quite relevant to other fields as well. Aimed primarily at those who will eventually be administering, planning, delivering, and evaluating programs, it strikes a balance between technical evaluation issues and the real-world settings in which evaluations are conducted. Covers historical development of program evaluation in the health care field and describes some contemporary influences. Discusses design of program components, the reliability and validity of individual measures, the advantages and disadvantages of different data collection methods, and basic data analysis approaches. Covers important administrative and political issues, and concludes with an analysis of the future role of evaluation in developing public policy for the delivery of health services.

Struening E. L. and M. Guttentag [eds.] *Handbook of evaluation research* (Vol. 1). Beverly Hills, CA: Sage, 1975.

Contains 21 papers on topics such as policy and strategy in evaluation research, design of evaluation studies, development and evaluation of measures, data collection through interviews and records, evaluation through social ecology, data analytic methods, and communicating evaluation results.

Suchman, E. A. *Evaluative research: Principles and practice in public service and social action programs.* New York: Russell Sage, 1967.

This was one of the first books to deal with the problems of doing evaluation research on public service and social action programs. Focuses on evaluation as a method for studying the effectiveness of any organized effort at planned social change, drawing examples from the field of public health. The book begins with a brief historical account and critique of evaluation efforts, followed by a conceptual analysis of the evaluation process. Covers methodological problems, research designs applicable to evaluation, and the measurement of program effects. Discusses administrative aspects such as the relationship between evaluation and program planning, demonstration, and operation. Analyzes barriers to evaluation and problems in administering evaluation studies. Concludes with a brief exposition on the relationship of evaluation research to social experimentation.

Weiss, C. H. *Evaluating action programs: Readings in social action and education.* Boston: Allyn & Bacon, 1972.

This book helps the evaluator in training understand the purposes of evaluation and the methods for obtaining information and reaching conclusions. An elementary knowledge of social science research methods is assumed. Avoiding prefabricated rules and instructions for evaluation, the book offers alternative strategies of design, measurement, and communication to accommodate existing constraints. Contributions of evaluators experienced in many fields show some areas of consensus across professional specialties.

Weiss, C. H. *Evaluation research: Methods for assessing program effectiveness.* Englewood Cliffs, NJ: Prentice-Hall, 1972.

Focuses on the structures within which evaluation takes place, as well as the methods and techniques suited to the evaluative task. Discusses the contributions of evaluation research to rational decision making, and the purposes, both acknowledged and unacknowledged, for which people decide to undertake program evaluation. Covers the fundamental issues of formulating program goals; measuring program inputs, intervening processes, and outcomes; and modes of data collection. Explains experimental, quasi-experimental, and nonexperimental designs, and considers the often neglected notion of comparative program evaluation. Analyzes settings that can create serious research problems and constraints that frequently limit the use of evaluation results.

EVALUATION QUESTIONS/STANDARDS

Fink, A. and J. Kosecoff. *How to: Evaluate education programs.* Arlington, Virginia: Capitol Publications; 1977-to present.

This series of monthly newsletters offers step-by-step instructions for practically the entire spectrum of evaluation activities. Designed for a relatively nontechnical audience, topics include how to: analyze program costs; use Delphi method; conduct a survey; use the normal curve; conduct an evaluability assessment; use computers to analyze evaluation data.

Tallmadge, G. K. *The joint dissemination panel ideabook.* Mountainview, CA: RMC Research Corporation, October 1972.

This monograph provides rigorous standards for performing evaluations. Among the questions it helps evaluators answer are: Did a change occur as a result of the program? Was the effect consistent and observed often enough to be statistically significant? Was the effect educationally significant? Can the intervention be implemented in another location with a reasonable expectation of comparable impact?

DESIGN AND SAMPLING

Alwin, D. F. *Survey design and analysis: Current issues.* Sage Contemporary Social Science Issues 46. Beverly Hills, CA: Sage, 1978.

This book focuses on survey-related issues and problems. These papers originally appeared as a special issue of *Sociological Methods & Research* in November 1977. Problems include: errors in surveys; effects of survey question wording and form; effects of interviewers' expectations; impact of informed consent regulations on response rate and response bias; patterns of response to mail surveys; treatment of missing data; and measurement errors.

Babbi, E. R. *The practice of social research* (2nd ed.). Belmont, CA: Wadsworth, 1979.

This book is an introduction to the logic and skills of social research. The contents are divided into four parts: I—An Introduction to Inquiry—explains what makes science different from other ways of knowing things, as preparation for viewing more specific aspects of research design and execution; II—The Structuring of Inquiry—covers the proper way to pose scientific questions by research design, measurement, and sampling; III—Modes of Observations—describes the various observational techniques available to social scientists; field research, content analysis, experiments, evaluation research, and survey research; and IV—Analysis of Data—discusses analyzing research data and understanding social phenomena.

Campbell, D. T. and J. C. Stanley. *Experimental and quasi-experimental designs for research.* Chicago: Rand McNally, 1963.

This is the classic text that introduces, discusses, and compares preexperimental, quasi-experimental, and true experimental research designs. All later discussions of these topics inevitably refer to this text, which discusses internal and external validity, and tests of significance for several research designs.

Cochran, W. G. *Sampling techniques* (3rd ed.). New York: John Wiley, 1977.

This text presents sampling theory as it has been developed for use in surveys. The emphasis is on theory, but numerous illustrations show how the theory is applied. Gives proofs of the more important theorems. The bulk of the text consists of mathematically sophisticated analyses of the most important sampling techniques, their variations and extensions.

Glass, G. V, L. Wilson, and J. H. Gottman *Design and analysis of time-series experiments.* Boulder: Colorado Associated University Press, 1975.

The authors analyze the basic time-series design by looking at variations of it and threats to its validity. Some mathematical sophistication is required.

Jessen, R. J. *Statistical survey techniques.* New York: John Wiley, 1978.

Describes sampling and other survey methodologies fundamental to many fields, and evaluates their properties. Each chapter introduces a survey principle or method by means of an example. Further developments of the method are described with numerical examples and some statistical analysis. Chapters conclude with review illustrations and their solutions. A Mathematical Notes section offers derivations and proofs of important terms and theorems. Analyzes important sampling techniques, discussing their advantages, weaknesses, and applicability in different situations. The final chapters deal with other survey techniques, such as coverage, canvassing, and measurement; and how to analyze and present results.

Shoemaker D. M. *Use of sampling with OSOE Title I evaluation models*. Washington, DC: Government Printing Office, 1979. Stock #1979 628-097-1992.

This handbook describes in easy-to-understand language a full range of sampling and design strategies for evaluators.

Rutman, L. [ed.] *Evaluation research methods: A basic guide*. Beverly Hills, CA: Sage, 1977.

Emphasizes conceptual and methodological issues peculiar to evaluations that attempt to determine and account for program effectiveness. Discusses the conditions a program must meet to allow evaluation, and analyzes two procedures for determining program "evaluability." Identifies some practical problems in measuring and attributing change to social intervention; focuses on experimental and quasi-experimental designs that provide high levels of internal validity; and discusses analytic procedures for handling data form nonexperimental designs. Describes a national experiment that tested alternative ways to get organizations to adopt a mental health patient-release program. Identifies factors related to adoption and suggests ways to increase the use of evaluation research findings. Concludes with a brief discussion of cost benefit analysis in evaluation.

Warwick, D. P. and C. A. Lininger. *The sample survey: Theory and practice*. New York: McGraw-Hill, 1975.

This text serves as an introduction to the theory and practice of sample surveys in concrete research settings. Critical issues include: (1) the need for intracultural as well as cross-cultural equivalence of surveys, (2) the political and ethical contexts of survey research, and (3) the importance of avoiding the survey method when other techniques are more appropriate. Introduces the basic quantitative concepts of the field without statistical and technical jargon. Begins with an introductory overview of the sample survey, then discusses details of planning and design, sampling and estimation, questionnaire design, the survey interview, organizing and administering fieldwork, editing and coding, and analysis and reporting.

Webb, E. J., D. T. Campbell, and R. D. Schwartz et al. *Unobtrusive measures: Nonreactive research in the social sciences*. Chicago: Rand McNally, 1966.

This monograph assumes that the goal of the social scientist is to obtain reliable comparisons, and this can be done by ruling out rival hypotheses that make comparisons ambiguous and tentative. With this in mind, the authors supplement common forms of measurement such as the interview and questionnaire, with unobtrusive measures that do not require the cooperation of a respondent and that do not themselves contaminate the response. They analyze three groups of unobtrusive measures: physical traces resulting from past behavior (e.g., natural erosion such as floor wear); archives (e.g., actuarial records, political and judicial records, written documents); and observations (e.g., exterior physical signs, expressive movement, language behavior).

Williams, B. *A sampler on sampling*. New York: John Wiley, 1978.

Explains concepts and principles of statistical sampling to the nonmathematical reader. Uses numerical examples from which generalizations are made. Less exhaustive than the typical text on sampling, it discusses only a few of the available sampling designs and has almost nothing about subsequent analyses of survey data. Most of the book is on sampling distributions—how they arise, how they are related to the confidence placed in a sample, and how they can be influenced by such things as sample size, method of calculating estimates, and sampling procedures.

MEASUREMENT

Cronbach, L. J. *Essentials of psychological testing.* (3rd ed.) New York: Harper & Row, 1970.

This book is an introduction to the field of psychometrics. It covers topics such as: who uses tests, purposes and types of tests, administering tests, scoring, test validation, ability testing, factor analysis, personnel selection, interest inventories, personality measurement, and judgments and observations.

Ebel, R. L. *Measuring educational achievement.* Englewood Cliffs, NJ: Prentice-Hall, 1965.

The varieties of educational achievement tests—their functions, problems, and solutions—are examined. Among the topics covered are what achievement tests should measure, how to plan a classroom test, describing test scores statistically, and how to improve test quality through item analysis.

Gronlund, N. E. *Constructing achievement tests.* Englewood Cliffs, NJ: Prentice-Hall, 1977.

This book on achievement tests contains important information on constructing essay tests and validity and reliability, and provides simplified methods of treating test scores.

Guilford, J. P. *Psychometric methods* (2nd ed.). New York: McGraw-Hill, 1954.

This is the classic test in psychometric methods, unifying the theory and calculations of psychological measurement. Discussion tends to be relatively sophisticated. Includes detailed analyses of scaling and measurement procedures, testing, reliability and validity, and factor analysis.

Nunnally, J. C. *Psychometric theory* (2nd ed.). New York: McGraw-Hill, 1978.

An introduction to the fundamentals of all psychological measurement methods. The emphasis throughout is on the theory of measurement rather than a summary of empirical findings. In general, mathematical developments are kept to a minimum with most technical aspects explained verbally.

Whitta, D. K. [ed.] *Handbook of measurement and assessment in behavioral sciences.* Reading, MA: Addison-Wesley, 1968.

A handbook and comprehensive reference on measurement procedures and problems that are intrinsic to research in the behavioral sciences. Much of the text is mathematically sophisticated, but the introduction gives a nonmathematical summary. Part I, on measurement statistics, covers statistical tests of group differences, analysis of covariance, multivariate analysis of variance, factor analysis, scaling, and sampling. Part II covers a wide range of applications of measurement and assessment techniques, including intelligence, aptitude and achievement, personality, creativity, interest, and guidance.

ANALYSIS OF INFORMATION

Amick, D. J. and H. J. Walberg [eds.] *Introductory multivariate analysis for educational, psychological, and social research.* Berkeley, CA: McCutchan, 1975.

The purpose of this book is to explain the applications, advantages, and disadvantages of those multivariate statistical techniques most frequently used in educational, psychological and social research. The book avoids advanced mathematics and computer techniques, concentrating instead on the purposes, assumptions and uses of the procedures. A basic knowledge of statistics is required, however.

Blalock, H. M. *Social statistics* (2nd ed.). New York: McGraw-Hill, 1972.

This text covers statistical techniques most useful in social research. It avoids mathematical derivations but discusses the underlying principles of all major techniques. Each topic includes a numerical example. The emphasis is on similarities among the most commonly used statistical tests and measures. Gives detailed, but relatively nonmathematical, discussions of descriptive (univariate) statistics, inferential and basic nonparametric statistics, simple analysis of variance, and regression and correlations. Also covers analysis of covariance and sampling.

Box, G.E.P., W. G. Hunter, and J. S. Hunter. *Statistics for experimenters: An introduction to design, data analysis, and model building.* New York: John Wiley, 1978.

Using simple statistics and mathematics, the authors introduce ideas and techniques they have found especially useful in collecting and analyzing data. This is an introduction to the philosophy of experimentation and the part that statistics plays. The emphasis is on thinking about the nature of the scientific problem itself, on analyzing data plots and other graphic displays, and on understanding statistical principles and their practical consequences. Examples are used throughout to illustrate principles and techniques.

Fisher, R. A. (Sir). *The design of experiments* (9th ed.). New York: Hafner, 1971.

This is the original text on experimental design, written by the pioneer of the concept. The emphasis is on designs used successfully in various applications (notably, agriculture) and the structure of these designs in relation to valid statistical inference. Valuable insights, but not an introductory text.

Gibbons, J. D. *Nonparametric methods for quantitative analysis.* New York: Holt, Rinehart & Winston, 1976.

This book introduces the basic principles of nonparametric statistics. Each technique begins with an example, followed by a step-by-step application of the procedure. This involves a statement of the problem or question, a description of the type of data and measurement needed, and an explanation of the statistical analysis. The book focuses on situations commonly faced by researchers and ones in which simple techniques can be employed.

Haack, D. G. *Statistical literacy: A guide to interpretation.* North Scituate, MA: Duxbury, 1979.

Without mathematical symbols or formulas, this book tells how to interpret statistics properly. Explanations are based on verbal and numerical examples, definitions, graphs, figures, and the like. Includes several topics not usually covered in an introductory statistics text, such as how to distinguish between meaningless numbers and credible statistics. Explains the proper use of statistics to describe a set of data and discusses statistical inference. Also covers common techniques of design of experiments, sample surveys, regression and correlation, and index numbers. A final chapter deals specifically with interpreting statistics relevant to epidemiology.

Harris, R. J. *A primer of multivariate statistics.* New York: Academic, 1975.

An introduction to the more common multivariate techniques for readers interested in research in sociology, psychology, and other social and behavioral sciences. Keeps mathematics to a minimum by concentrating on heuristic descriptions of what the math is really designed to accomplish. Sections with higher-than-normal levels of mathematics are so noted. Includes detailed discussions of six common multivariate procedures: multiple regression, discriminant analysis, multivariate analysis of variance, canonical correlation, principal component analysis, and factor analysis. Concludes with a review of matrix algebra and a discussion of canned statistical computer programs.

Hauser, P. M. *Social statistics in use.* New York: Russell Sage, 1975.

Explains why social statistics, especially those collected and compiled by government, are important, and how they are used in the public interest. Emphasizes the relationship between social statistics and policy development, both in the public and private sectors. The uses of (social) statistical data are analyzed according to the user's general and specific purposes and by classification of the user's business or area of interest. In between an introductory chapter on "Why statistics?" and a concluding chapter on social indicators, the following social statistics are discussed: population, births, deaths, and health; marriage, divorce and the family; education; the labor force; Social Security and welfare; delinquency and crime; consumption and the consumer; housing and construction; metropolitan transport and land use; outdoor recreation; governments; elections; and public opinion polls.

Johnson A. *Social statistics without tears*. New York: McGraw-Hill, 1977.

Helps the reader understand basic statistical language, techniques, and principles well enough to evaluate the literature critically. Emphasizes classic statistical methods devoid of mathematics and technical jargon. Uses numerical examples. Part one of the book discusses measurement, distributions and tables, summary statistics, elementary probability theory, relationships and associations between two variables, basic multivariate analysis, and first-order relationships of more than two variables. Part two covers the fundamental concepts of sampling, estimation, and hypothesis testing. Concludes with an extensive glossary of terms and symbols.

Kirk, R. E. *Experimental design: Procedures for the behavioral sciences*. Belmont, CA: Brooks/Cole, 1968.

This text fills the gap between books that emphasize the statistical theory underlying experimental design and those that cover only the most elementary designs. With a minimum of mathematics, the text covers both elementary and complex designs and techniques available to behavioral scientists. Each experimental design begins with a research problem and computational example. Although proofs and derivations are avoided, the assumptions underlying each design are explicitly stated. Uses the same numerical data, with minor modifications, in different hypothetical situations throughout the book. After chapters on statistical inference and analysis of variance, the remainder of the book discusses and analyzes a wide range of simple and advanced experimental designs.

Nie, N., H. Hull, and J. G. Jenkins et al. *Statistical package for the social sciences* (2nd ed.). New York: McGraw-Hill, 1975.

SPSS is a system of computer programs designed for the analysis of social science data. Extremely useful for evaluation studies, this book tells you how to organize your data for analysis and how to set them up and read the results for a variety of techniques, such as descriptive statistics, contingency tables, correlation, regression, ANOVA, covariation, discriminant, and factor analysis.

Patton, M. O. *Qualitative evaluation methods*. Beverly Hills, CA: Sage, 1980.

This is a handbook for the collection and analysis of qualitative data and a theoretical treatise on the nature and value of alternative evaluation models. Among the topics that are addressed are the range of options, the nature of qualitative data, and the relationship between qualitative methods and behavioral objective approaches.

Siegel, S. *Nonparametric statistics for the behavioral sciences.* New York: McGraw-Hill, 1956.

Introduces all nonparametric (distribution-free) statistical techniques useful to analysis in the behavioral sciences and notes the type of data to which each is applicable. Gives the rationale underlying the test and example of its application and compares it to similar tests. An appendix contains all necessary statistical tables.

Tatsuoka, M. M. *Multivariate analysis: Techniques for educational and psychological research.* New York: John Wiley, 1971.

This text presents a series of multivariate statistical techniques for the mathematically sophisticated reader. Emphasis is on development of the procedures and their properties; however, rigorous mathematical proofs and derivations are held to a minimum. Clarity is enhanced by identifying analogies between given multivariate techniques and the corresponding univariate methods. The book offers rigorous reviews of matrix algebra and multiple regression, followed by the development of: analysis of covariance, multivariate significance tests of group differences, discriminant analysis and canonical correlation, multivariate analysis of variance and classification problems.

Tukey, J. W. *Exploratory data analysis.* Reading, MA: Addison-Wesley, 1977.

This text explains a new approach to data analysis pioneered by the author, which he believes to be more effective than conventional statistical methods. Through a set of fast, straightforward, and mainly intuitive techniques, it extracts patterns, exceptions to patterns, and hypotheses out of a body of data. It is a numerical approach, depending on simple arithmetic and easy-to-draw "pictures." Difficult formulas and mathematics are not part of the analysis. The book introduces, discusses, and applies the various exploratory techniques, using numerical examples.

Ullman, N. R. *Elementary statistics: An applied approach.* New York: John Wiley, 1978.

Presents and clarifies the purposes and concepts of introductory statistics for nonmathematical readers. All techniques are explained by examples and numerical problems. The emphasis is on application rather than on theory and development. The contents include presentations of descriptive statistics, probability and common distributions, sampling and inferential statistics, some nonparametric methods, regression and correlation, and analysis of variance.

Winer, B. J. *Statistical principles in experimental design* (2nd ed.). New York: McGraw-Hill, 1971.

This well-known book is a text and reference source on the statistical principles underlying experimental design. Particular emphasis is given to designs that are likely to prove useful in research in the behavioral sciences. In general, mathematical derivations and proofs are avoided with all designs and concepts analyzed in terms of numerical examples and computational formulas. After a brief review of elementary statistics, the book presents detailed analyses of all common designs and their variants. Briefly discusses multivariate techniques related to analysis of variance.

Zeller, R. A. and E. G. Carmines. *Statistical analysis of social data.* Chicago: Rand McNally, 1978.

Introduces the techniques of statistical analysis of social data. The authors use a single example (analysis of the popularity of Harry Truman) throughout the volume to illustrate the various procedures. The book is divided into two major parts. Part I discusses all major aspects of descriptive statistics including frequencies, central tendency and variability, categorical variables, comparison of means, and bivariate and multivariate correlation and regression. Part II presents the fundamentals of statistical inference, beginning with introductions to sampling, types of inference, and probability theory. Inferential procedures are presented for categorical variables, means, and regression and correlation coefficients. The last chapter discusses advanced capabilities of multiple regression. Appendices include glossaries of statistical terms and formulas.

WRITING AND REPORTING

Day, R. A. *How to write and publish a scientific paper.* Philadelphia: ISI Press, 1979.

Although concerned primarily with scientific papers, many of the chapters in this book are essential reading for evaluators. Among them: use and misuse of English, avoiding jargon, how to write the introduction, results and discussion, how to prepare the literature cited, and how to design tables and prepare illustrations.

Katzer, J., K. H. Cook, and W. W. Crounch. *Evaluating information: A guide for users of social science research.* Reading, MA: Addison-Wesley, 1978.

Explains how to evaluate research reports. Mostly devoted to the principles underlying criteria and for evaluation, using what the authors refer to as an "error model" of research. Each chapter leads to several specific questions one must ask of a research report, followed by a step-by-step guide for evaluation using these questions. Aimed at nonresearchers, the book avoids many of the technical terms and statistical formulas normally found in research texts.

King, L. S. *Why not say it clearly? A guide to scientific writing.* Boston: Little, Brown, 1978.

This book is a primer for science writers. Several topics covered are good and bad writing, editing and revising, and style analysis. The author gives examples of good science writing and provides hints for clarity.

Leggett, G., C. D. Mead, and W. Charvat. *Prentice-Hall handbook for writers* (7th ed.). Englewood Cliffs, NJ: Prentice-Hall, 1978.

A basic guide to the use of standard English: the sentence (phrases, clauses); case; tense and mood; adjectives and adverbs; diagramming; sentence fragments; comma splice; faulty agreement; faulty reference of pronouns; shifts in point of view; dangling modifiers; awkward sentences; manuscript forms; numbers; abbreviations; syllabication;

end punctuation; internal punctuation; word punctuation; the whole composition; paragraphs; logic; words (dictionary, vocabulary); the library; summaries and examinations; business letters and grammatical terms.

Strunk, W. and E. B. White. *The elements of style.* New York: Macmillan, 1962.

Provides basic information on the elementary rules of usage, compositions, form, and style.

University of Chicago Press. *A manual of style* (12th ed.). University of Chicago Press, 1969.

Important reading for evaluators is included in the chapter on style; also a primer for English punctuation, spelling, names and terms, numbers, equations, illustrations, captions, and legends, tables, mathematics in types, abbreviations, notes and footnotes, bibliographies, citing public documents and indexes.

REFERENCES

BERDIE, D. R. and J. F. ANDERSON (1974) Questionnaires: Design and Use. Metuchen, NJ: Scarecrow.

BLOOM, B. S. (1956) Taxonomy of Educational Objectives: Cognitive Domain. New York: David McKay.

CAMPBELL, D. T. and J. C. STANLEY (1963) Experimental and Quasi-Experimental Designs for Research. Chicago: Rand McNally.

CARO, F. G. [ed.] (1971) Readings in Evaluation Research. New York: Russell Sage.

COCHRAN, W. G. (1977) Sampling Techniques. New York: John Wiley.

CRONBACH, L. G. et al. (1980) Toward Reform of Program Evaluation. San Francisco: Jossey-Bass.

DONABEDIAN, A. (1969) A Guide to Medical Care Administration. Vol. 2: Medical Care Appraisal. New York: American Public Health Association.

DUNN, W. N., I. I. MITROFF, and S. J. DEUTSCH (1981) "The obsolescence of evaluation research." Evaluation and Program Planning 4, 3/4: 207-218.

EBEL, R. L. (1972) Essentials of Educational Measurement. Englewood Cliffs, NJ: Prentice-Hall.

FINK, A. and J. KOSECOFF (1978) An Evaluation Primer. Beverly Hills, CA: Sage.

GRONLUND, N. E. (1977) Constructing Achievement Tests. Englewood Cliffs, NJ: Prentice-Hall.

GLASS, G. V, L. WILLSON, and J. H. GOTTMAN (1972) Design and Analysis of Time Series Experiments. Boulder: Laboratory of Educational Research, University of Colorado.

GUTTENTAG, M. and E. L. STRUENING [eds.] (1975) Handbook of Evaluation Research. Beverly Hills, CA: Sage.

Joint Committee on Standards for Educational Evaluation (1981) Standards for Evaluations of Educational Programs, Projects, and Materials. New York: McGraw-Hill.

KING, L. S. (1978) why Not Say It Clearly? A Guide to Scientific Writing. Boston: Little, Brown.

KOSECOFF, J., A. FINK, J. CULLEN, et al. (1982) "Guidelines for evaluating cancer control programs." Preventive Medicine 11: 187-198.

LIKERT, R. (1932) "A technique for the measurement of attitudes." Archives of Psychology, No. 40.

NEDELSKY, L. (1954) "Absolute grading standards for objective tests." Educational and Psychological Measurement 14: 3-19.

OSGOOD, C. E., G. J. SUCI, and P. H. TANNENBAUM (1957) The Measurement of Meaning. Urbana: University of Illinois Press.

PATTON, M. Q. (1980) Qualitative Evaluation Methods. Beverly Hills, CA: Sage.

PAYNE, D. (1974) The Assessment of Learning. Lexington, MA: D. C. Heath.

RIECKEN, H. W. and R. F. BORUCH [eds.] (1974) Social Experimentation: A Method for Planning and Evaluating Social Interventions. New York: Academic.

ROSSI, P. H. and H. E. FREEMAN (1982) Evaluation: A Systematic Approach. Beverly Hills, CA: Sage.

SATCHER, D., J. KOSECOFF, and A. FINK (1980) "Results of a needs assessment strategy in developing a family practice program in an inner-city community." Journal of Family Practice 10, 5: 871-879.

SCRIVEN, M. (1967) "The methodology of evaluation," in R. E. Stake (ed.) Curriculum Evaluation. American Educational Research Association Monograph Series on Evaluation No. 1. Chicago: Rand McNally.

SHOEMAKER, D. M. (1979) Use of Sampling with the USOE Title I Evaluation Models. Washington, DC: Government Printing Office.

SIEGEL, S. (1956) Nonparametric Statistics for the Behavioral Sciences. New York: McGraw-Hill.

TALLMADGE, B. W. (1977) The Joint Dissemination Panel Ideabook. Mountainview, CA: RMC Research Corp.

TUCKMAN, G. B. (1972) Conducting Educational Research, New York: Harcourt Brace Jovanovich.

U.S. General Accounting Office (1978) Assessing Social Program Impact Evaluations: A Checklist Approach. Washington, DC: Government Printing Office.

WEISS, C. H. (1972) Evaluation Research. Englewood Cliffs, NJ: Prentice-Hall.